VICTOR CHANG

VICTOR CHANG

A Tribute to My Father

VANESSA CHANG

PAN
Pan Macmillan Australia

First published 2001 in Pan by Pan Macmillan Australia Pty Limited
St Martins Tower, 31 Market Street, Sydney

Reprinted 2001 (twice)

National Library of Australia
cataloguing-in-publication data:

Chang, Vanessa.
Victor Chang: a tribute to my father.

ISBN 0 330 36322 0.

1. Chang, Victor. 2. Surgeons—Australia—Biography.
3. Fathers—Australia—Biography. I. Title.

617.0232092

Typeset in 13/16 Adobe Garamond by Post Pre-press Group
Printed in Australia by McPherson's Printing Group

For my father, I miss you.
For my mother, with love.

Contents

Acknowledgments

I would like to thank the following people for their contributions to this book and for their support in helping to achieve a very tight deadline: Ann Chang, Matthew Chang, Marcus Chang, Aunty Fung and Uncle Reg Young, Dr Mark Shanahan, Pearl Hansen, Dr Saw Huat Seong, Peter Lee, Uncle Les Chang, Dr Michael Allam, Sister Bernice, Dr Rama Rao, Rosina Johnston, Neville Wran, Tom Hayson, Bill Lee, Sha-mayne Chan, Michael Munro, Emma Quick, Professor Michael O'Rourke, Fiona Coote, Professor Don Harrison, John Gossage, Dr Guan and Dr Margaret Chong, Murray Clapham, Frank Tamru, Michael McBride, Professor Mitsuo Umezu, Dr Bernard Ee, Marjorie Burnett, Helen Gosper, Phil Spratt, Julie Meldrum, Margaret Vella and David West. I would also like to thank the authors of the letters sent to my family, whether published in this tribute or unpublished.

Preface

I know my father better now, after having written this book, than I ever knew him, which is a sad and strange feeling. As I write this preface, I am still discovering more information about his life and hearing stories that have not reached my ears until now. No doubt there is so much more to learn, and if I were to include it all, this book would probably never be published.

In 1992, a year after my father's death and still suffering deeply from the shock of its sudden and horrific manner, I considered writing a book about his life. Somehow, the idea of this book came to the attention of a few people outside my family circle and soon I was receiving letters from around this nation encouraging me to 'write that book'. Although I did begin doing a little preliminary research back in 1992, when it came to the crunch, I was unable to set my mind to it. It was too soon after his death and the pain, which remains today but to a lesser degree, paralysed me and rendered me incapable of reliving the memories. I was only 22.

According to the *Oxford Dictionary* a 'tribute' is 'something said, done, or given as a mark of respect or affection'. That is why 'tribute' is a fitting description for this book; it is my tribute to my father. Writing it has been one of the loneliest and most confrontational experiences of my life. I have produced a short biography in which I hope to share a little of my father's life experience—both personal and public, with the help of other contributors.

July 4, 2001 marks the tenth year that has passed since that bitterly cold day in 1991. I am 32 years old and I am stunned that the years have passed so rapidly.

I have relied on the memories of many people in my father's life to complete this picture. Also, from the thousands of letters my family received after Dad died, I have selected what I thought was a good representation of the bulk of the letters from people around the world—the letters ultimately motivated me to write this book.

Finally, I'm sure that many people are still inquisitive about the exact circumstances of my father's death, how it happened, who did it, whether they are still in jail and when they will get out. I have not written about this; as I've said, this is a tribute to his life.

All royalties earnt from the purchase of this book will go to the Victor Chang Cardiac Research Institute.

Vanessa Chang
July 2001

Eulogy

I thank God that I had the chance on many occasions to accompany my father at some obscure hour in the night to St Vincent's to watch him perform open-heart surgery.

When I was very young, people would always ask me whether I intended to follow in the footsteps of Dad and become a heart surgeon, and too many times I vehemently denied that I would do such a thing. It was probably only four or five years ago that I was able to enter the operating theatre and watch Dad perform a valve replacement, and it was only at that time that I realised what a skilful and brilliant man he was.

His hands moved so effortlessly and tenderly over the patient's heart. It seemed as though it was second nature to him, and when breath was brought to the body, I remember my father's smiling face as he proudly announced to me: 'See how easy it is, Ness. You can do that, can't you?'

And I understand now as I did at that moment why they call Dad a magician, a miracle worker and a man who worked through God with his two precious hands, and it makes me so proud knowing that Dad was able to give new life to so many people here today.

Dad dedicated his life to endeavouring to give life, and I can't find the words to explain how I am aching now . . . now that he has been snatched from us all.

I adored him as a man, I respected and admired him as a master surgeon, but most of all I loved him as a father, and I feel blessed that I was able to share 22 years of my life with him, in which time I have acquired a wealth of the most beautiful memories which fortunately can never be erased.

My family has received literally hundreds of letters and phone calls, pouring in every day from all over the world; our house has been transformed into a garden. I am just so touched when I see what an impact my father made in Australia and, indeed, all over the world. I didn't know that so many people cared so much. You can imagine how my family and those friends who are especially close to Dad, the people that were able to see him in his home environment, will grieve his death for ever more, and I thank you all for thinking so much about us at this time.

Dad was a real character . . . the jet-black hair, the button nose and bushy brows, the gold-rimmed glasses. He was only five foot eight, but his personality towered above that, perhaps because he was such a charismatic and strong person. He wasn't forceful but he had power and great resolve, and ambition beyond belief. Nothing was too far from reach; anything was possible.

I guess what I am trying to say is that he was a supreme optimist, and luckily he was able to pass that down to my mother and myself, Matthew and Marcus, and a lot of us here, I think. Dad's famous grin was often accompanied by an hilarious staccato chuckle, the crinkling eyes and the grasping of stomach muscles.

At home Dad would walk around, clad in his shaggy cut-off jeans, dark blue T-shirt, slippers and, of course, the famous beanie—offering to clean every car that entered the driveway. After that, a coffee at Bar Coluzzi, which he regarded as the closest Sydney would ever get to Italy. Perhaps a movie accompanied by a good cigar and, finally, a fantastic Chinese meal at Bill Lee's—everyone was invited. And that's just a glimpse of what happened outside the operating theatre.

But personally, my father has always symbolised hope and success for me. He was encouraging and consoling, and whilst he wasn't always at home 24 hours of the day I knew that he was loving me and taking care of my family in his own way.

Dad adored people and he has a few of what he called 'adopted sons and a daughter' who are the closest friends of my brothers and me. Dad was a great provider, a provider of support, a provider of love, a provider of life and a provider of fond memories.

I'll miss him terribly. There is consolation in knowing that he has been immortalised in those of you whose life he touched and in the memories of those who will love him eternally.

A little Chinese nun told me that he is surely a saint in heaven and I can just imagine Dad in his beanie now, grinning down with those white teeth and patting me on the head and saying, 'Ness, everything will work out.'

Vanessa Chang
July 1991

1

Small hands

I am having difficulty breathing, so I repeat my mantra: 'In through the nose, out through the mouth.' Am I succeeding in convincing myself? What's all that yellow fluid? I contemplate its appearance; is it blood? I wonder. It couldn't be, the scalpel hasn't even touched the skin yet . . . very messy business. I don't think I can watch this bit, the last time I saw a scalpel slide through flesh I *did* faint and that was only a small procedure, not like this one. Suddenly Dad looks at me, all I can see are his almond eyes. 'You OK, Ness?' he asks. I just nod; at this point I'm not sure whether I am or not, so better to play safe and tell him I'm fine. He can only see my eyes anyway, not the grimace I can feel forming on my mouth. I am fourteen years old.

There, done, no more scalpel, amazingly there isn't too much blood. Ryobi. The drill is louder than I expected it to be. It cuts vertically down the centre of the breastbone—this is too much. Cold metal. A self-retaining retractor is clamped on either side of the freshly sawed bone and wound to separate each side of the chest and keep it apart. No wonder patients are so sore when they wake up; it's not the internal work that hurts, it's all the cracking and sawing that goes on outside, before the actual operation on the heart.

The smell is bitter, like sulphur, and makes my nose twitch. I watch the fumes rise to the ceiling; this is what burning flesh and bone smells like. I venture to ask Dad what he is doing with what appears to be a soldering iron. He says he's stopping the wound from bleeding; cauterising it. All around the theatre I see friendly eyes peering up at me; do they think I'm going to faint, or are they trying to decide whether I look like my Dad. Shouldn't they be concentrating on what they're doing?

The mask is hot around my face and the cap keeps slipping down. Dad seems comfortable but I can hardly relax. I had a friend with me tonight but he turned green and broke into a cold sweat, so he was led out of theatre for a cup of tea. I stayed on.

The patient's head is at my knees, I'm standing on a little stool, too scared to move, or even to breathe in case I knock anything over. I sneak a feel of the patient's forehead and quickly withdraw my hand, shocked at how cold and hard it is, like a smooth stone that's been sitting at the bottom of an ice-cold pond. This guy's lucky he doesn't know what's going on, I think to myself.

Now the man is completely covered in green drapes.

I can only see a little red window—a window to this man's soul? No, it's just his heart; this is where Dad will operate.

There's a vast array of equipment in the room. Various machines click and beep, talking to their owners about the condition of the patient; the anaesthetist alone has a whole range of machines just for his job: to deliver drugs and gases, for taking pressures and blood samples, for monitoring the patient's vital signs and responses. I see several video screens suspended from the ceiling; everyone will be looking up to check them throughout the operation. The monster near me is the heart–lung machine, large, complex and vital to the success of this type of heart operation. Occasionally Dad talks to the theatre staff, calm and collected. I'm embarrassed because he keeps asking me questions. The nurses giggle too. Dad is joking around.

It's very quiet. As Dr Harry Windsor, Dad's mentor and the first Australian doctor to perform a heart transplant, observed, 'The best operating rooms are almost eerily quiet, relieved by the occasional sally; only efficiency produces such an atmosphere. There is no place for showmanship, good work is obvious.'

Every now and then Dad calls someone's name to ask how this or that is looking. It's amazing that he is so familiar with all those metal instruments, trays of them; they all look the same to me. That one looks particularly nasty, though. I wonder what it does. Dad once told me that he dropped his spectacles inside a patient and they never found them. I know that can't be true because they do a thorough count of every swab that's placed inside the body during the operation; I must take him up on that when he's finished. My feet look funny, puffy in blue surgical slippers. Time: 1.00 am. It's cold in here. Dad announces that he's ready to go. Let the magic begin.

My father once explained the reason he was a successful surgeon to his friend, St Vincent's official photographer John Gosage. He said his hands were so small that he was able to get into places where no other surgeons could reach. I laughed when John related this to me. Of course Dad was joking, as he always did when he couldn't give someone a serious answer.

He was asked a similar question in an interview during a visit to Singapore as a guest of then prime minister Lee Kuan Yew. The interviewer, a doctor, asked what qualities Dad was looking for when he selected trainees. Dad answered:

You have to look for a person who has all the attributes of a good surgeon: someone who is dexterous, who has a solid intellectual grasp of the arts of cardiac surgery, and who is highly motivated and is completely dedicated to his work. That type of person usually has a driving personality, [he is] an achiever and a leader. However, to develop a reputation he has to realise that it cannot be done overnight. It will take time and it is his job to be able to deliver the goods. That is, produce good results again and again.

From a young age, Dad knew medicine was his calling, but he didn't always know it was cardiothoracic surgery he was destined for. In high school, a vocational officer had advised him that he should study engineering or medicine and that if he chose medicine, he should think about specialising in the treatment of cancer—to help people who contract the illness that killed his mother.

By the time he reached university he felt this was an overcrowded field and he was more interested in studying either the brain or the heart. In the mid 1960s he told my mother, Ann Chang, that he had once considered neurosurgery as a possibility. After studying the subject for one term, however, he changed his mind because he thought it was too depressing. He was referring to his experience of having to write out death certificates too often and the harrowing effect it had upon him. As he explained to Mum, with cardiac surgery the progress of patients from near dead to almost full recovery in a short period was both dramatic and inspiring.

Marjorie Burnett, Dad's friend from high school, distinctly remembers asking him what branch of medicine he was thinking about specialising in. She would often see him pop his head around the door at the Angus & Robertson bookstore where she worked. He was not well off as a student so would order his medical books through Marjorie to take advantage of her staff discount. Dad told her that he was undecided between heart and gynaecology. Marjorie suggested that he should 'go for heart' because there seemed to be more gynaecology textbooks on the shelves in comparison to heart. When she reminded him of this conversation years later, however, he was surprised and didn't remember having been interested in gynaecology.

I introduced two student doctors, friends of mine, to Dad, and he questioned them on what they were thinking of specialising in when they finished university. When one of them mentioned gynaecology, my father looked at him with a stern smirk and advised that this specialty was a smelly job—I think my friend was disappointed and recently I discovered that he is now a surgeon.

Whatever specialty Dad was considering when he started studying medicine, it would be the heart that ultimately captured his attention and remained a source of fascination to him for the rest of his career. The work of the late Dr Harry Windsor and cardiac surgeon, Dr Mark Shanahan, also provided the inspiration he needed to convince him that heart surgery would call upon his skills and afford the challenges he craved.

Dad's first exposure to St Vincent's Hospital was in 1958, during his 'clinical years'. That is, when he was still attending lectures at university but was spending most of his time in the hospital obtaining practical experience and skills. In these first years, the young Victor Chang was introduced to three people at St

Vincent's who would become major influences in his life; all would remain close friends and mentors. Two, whom I have just mentioned, were Harry and Mark. The other was Sister Bernice. Her almost maternal friendship with my father was unique. She was, and still is, a powerful figure at St Vincent's and is revered by many, doctors and patients alike.

In 1960 Dad was living in the hospital grounds in a little cottage with other medical students. Sister Bernice remembers him as a lonely young man, wanting to make great headway in the world so that he could practise medicine. After his graduation in 1962, Dad became a junior resident medical doctor at St Vincent's, working in casualty. He would often visit Bernice for a chat, something that he would continue to do all his life, and despite not being a religious man, would never forget to ask her to say a little prayer for his patients. This led to his unofficial status in the hospital as an 'honorary Catholic'.

I grew up in awe of Sister Bernice; she has a reassuring touch and a strong, persuasive presence, a quality that is not quite of this world. She is also a keen observer of the human condition and made this observation about Dad and his relationship with his patients:

> There was something very special about [Victor], he had a real insight into how people felt, especially his patients when they were sick, and they all loved him for that. He tried to visit his patients once or twice through the day and try to settle them down. He was

one of the most outstanding medical men that I have ever dealt with. [He was] a very good, ethical man and people felt that when he was talking to them. He would bring his language down to their level to explain what would be happening during the operation, how they would progress and how they would be helped. He would explain the X-rays to them whether they wanted it or not, and this gave patients great confidence. He was also wonderfully good to the staff, they all loved him too.

Dr Mark Shanahan, who is now retired and living in Merimbula on the south coast of New South Wales, was working in the cardiothoracic unit at St Vincent's in October 1963. Harry Windsor was a close work colleague, and a man to whom both my father and Mark would ultimately owe so much of their success. Mark had been overseas for six years for his postgraduate training in London and New York, and was the first of the new generation of surgeons to have had such formal training in heart surgery.

One evening Mark gave a talk to the residents, after which he was approached by a student, 27-year-old Victor Chang, who introduced himself as 'a junior resident at the hospital'. It was his first year as a doctor. Mark says he was an unusual-looking fellow, with a fresh face and quite big ears.

The young doctor said to him, 'I'd really like to do what you've done.' Mark recalls that Victor appeared to be very young and somewhat naïve and inexperienced, but he seemed eager to hear of Dr Shanahan's experiences. Most surprising to Mark, Dad asked him what he thought about the future of cardiac surgery. In retrospect, Mark realised that the young Victor was already showing a vision of the future for which he would become quite famous. To assist his progress, Mark arranged for Dad to be one of only two senior residents to work in his unit in 1964.

Dad's first encounter with Harry Windsor was not as pleasant. Dad made a poor impression on him when he failed to turn up for his first shift—there had been some confusion in the weekend roster. Harry wondered about Mark's enthusiasm for this new senior resident and at first was not impressed. This soon changed, as Mark explained to me:

It wasn't long, however, before Harry was also won over as I had been, by Victor's charm, sincerity and efficiency. This achievement was indeed a credit to him as Harry was a tough taskmaster who expected nothing less than complete dedication and commitment. It also became evident that Victor had dexterity and technical skill equal to his proven academic ability. For this reason it was only a few months into his training that I encouraged him to undertake a right lower lobectomy of the lung which I expected to be easy. It proved, however, to be very difficult and Harry was keen for me to take over the operation. Victor, on the other hand, in spite of having two senior men watching his every move,

9

showed his characteristic self-confidence and was happy to continue. It was fortunate that I allowed him to do so for he completed the task skilfully and successfully. It was then that Harry and I both knew that we had the opportunity to influence and mould the career of a future colleague.

Dr Windsor became a great promoter of Dad's work, in fact one of Dad's fellow residents at the time, Dr Michael Allam, told me that Dad was commonly referred to as 'Harry's white-haired boy'. Dr Windsor, despite first impressions, was extremely taken by the young Victor Chang and helped him with his post-graduate training in cardiac surgery, and supported him with all his applications to the various hospitals overseas.

In September 1965, after two and a half years as resident medical officer, six months of which he had spent as surgical registrar to the cardiothoracic unit, Dad left Australia for what would be a total of six years of training at well-known and respected hospitals in England and the United States.

His first port of call was England. On the recommendation of Mark Shanahan, he continued his surgical training under Mark's own mentor, Aubrey York Mason, at St Anthony's Hospital in Cheam, Surrey. A South African-born general surgeon, Mason was regarded as one of the world's finest general surgeons. Over the years Dad formed the opinion that Mason was the most technically gifted surgeon he had ever known.

He was a great teacher and, as Mark Shanahan noted, he 'favoured colonials as his trainees'. He happily agreed to take Victor on board. The first six months of Dad's training was as a senior house officer in surgery and he later became a surgical registrar at St Anthony's.

Although my father worked hard to impress Aubrey York Mason and gain as much experience as he could, he did have time for recreation. During his brief stint at St Anthony's, he met a lovely Surrey girl. Her name was Ann Simmons, my mother, but that is a tale in itself.

In that same year he obtained his FRCS—Fellowship of the Royal College of Surgeons—in the company of Michael Allam. Michael, along with Dad and a small group of graduates from Hong Kong and Malaysia, supported each other in wintry London, studying night and day to pass their exams.

Michael remembers that they would often meet in the evening for short breaks and discussions. One of their favourite topics was the latest James Bond film. Their detailed knowledge of the cars and adventures of Bond was incredible and was regurgitated with bullet-like speed, one fellow trying to outdo the other in recalling facts. Often the need for a Chinese snack at night would see them visiting a noodle store—college food was not particularly appetising. About those times, Michael also said:

When Victor first arrived in London he took delivery of a new MGB roadster . . . We had our weekly Sunday foray to Soho for a Chinese lunch at Lee Ho

Fook restaurant in Gerard Street. The Hong Kong boys were more adept at using chopsticks, and polished off two to three bowls of rice to my one. The meal usually cost 10 shillings or less each. Then, if it was a nice day we'd drive to the Prospect of Whitby in the East End for a drink. I don't think Victor even drank alcohol, at least not regularly.

At St Anthony's Michael Allam saw first-hand Victor's manual dexterity. 'It was a joy to see someone using his hands so well who had graduated only two years earlier. In later years, he would tell me with a chuckle that he didn't need an operating microscope doing cardiac surgery because he purposefully had his spectacle lenses under-corrected.'

Dad left St Anthony's in 1966 and continued working under Dr York Mason at a different hospital, St Helier, in Surrey. He took with him a reference from the medical superintendent at St Anthony's which verified the period he spent at that hospital. The reference noted in an understated manner, as is the English way, that 'Dr Chang's work was uniformly excellent.' Dad trained at St Helier until September 1968 but, in the interim, he had been busy charming Ann Simmons, courting her tenaciously. He had convinced her to marry him and the two were expecting me, their first child, due in May 1969. When I was born Dad was working as surgical registrar at the famous Brompton Chest Clinic in London with Lord Brock and other notable surgeons. He was still there when my brother Matthew came into the world in October 1970. In 1970, when an opportunity to complete his thoracic surgical training at the Mayo Clinic in Minnesota became available, our family moved to the United States.

Harry Windsor had strong friendships with some of the doctors at the Mayo Clinic and he had arranged a year of residency for Dad. A letter from Harry to Dad in January 1970 says: 'I have had considerable correspondence with Mayo Clinic on your behalf. I think it is probably the best job in the US.' This opportunity provided the perfect avenue for Dad to complete his training.

Aubrey York Mason had visited St Vincent's in Sydney in 1968 and spoke to Mark Shanahan in glowing terms of Victor as a surgeon and as a man whom he felt was destined for distinction. The tributes from the Mayo Clinic were no less glowing and his reference from there, which Mark read back then with some awe, described Dad as one of the finest residents to work in its department in recent history.

By the time Dad and his new family reached Rochester, Minnesota, in December 1970, he had almost completed his thoracic training. The freezing cold weather in Minnesota made a lasting impression on both my parents because whenever they reminisced about the place, they would always preface with, 'It was the coldest place on earth . . .' My parents quickly became friendly with their host family, Guan and Margaret Chong. The Mayo Clinic had assigned the Chongs to the Changs. This was part of a system of mentoring for newly arrived residents of the clinic. Guan's tasks were to ensure that Mum, Dad and the family settled into life in Rochester without any hiccups.

For the first half of his stay, Dad worked with Dr Dwight McGoon, a brilliant cardiac surgeon, famous at the Mayo as a doctor with the most skilful and technically the most delicate touch, as he repaired complex congenital deformities of the heart in little babies and young children.

As he seemed to do with so many people over his lifetime, Dad endeared himself to Dwight McGoon, despite, as Guan Chong noted, their markedly different personalities. Dwight McGoon was serious, tactful, cool and calm, and controlled in a crisis. He was also a kind, fatherly gentleman who had to give up surgery prematurely when he was stricken by Parkinson's disease at the peak of his career. Guan Chong says Dad's exuberance in cardiac surgery was infectious when he was in training. He was an extrovert and never ceased to marvel at the new techniques he had learnt from McGoon.

In 1971, when Dad was a fellow at the Mayo, Henry Kissinger met Chinese leader Zhou En Lai and started 'Ping Pong' diplomacy—the exchange of knowledge between the two nations. In line with Kissinger's policy, the Mayo Clinic organised to train surgeons from around Asia. Guan tells a lovely story of the three Chinese men at the Mayo from three very different backgrounds: Victor Chang, an Australian Chinese; Guan Chong, a Chinese Malaysian; and Ernesto Ching, a Philippino Chinese. He said they became known as 'the Ching-Chong-Chang trio', confusing many consultants, despite the fact that they were all very different in appearance. The three of them became such an established part of the Mayo's history that people there continued to confuse the three, even after Dad's death in 1991.

Before he left for the US, Dad must have expressed his concern to Harry Windsor about the availability of jobs for himself back home at St Vincent's. Harry, loyal as ever to Dad's career, responded that he needn't worry about sacrificing opportunities in Australia for the US, saying, 'I don't think you need worry about something being available, but keep it to yourself. Just get all the experience you can.' I'm sure Dad was unaware that before he returned to Australia, Harry had already sought advice from a work colleague about Dad's appointment to the hospital. Harry was concerned that the nuns may not approve a person who was not a believer in the Christian or Jewish God.

By the end of 1971, Dad had been offered a permanent role at the Mayo Clinic. However, after one cold year in Minnesota with the family, he was ready to return to Sydney to pick up the scalpel again and work with Mark and Harry. The two surgeons had decided that they wanted to create a role for Dad to work alongside them at St Vincent's as staff cardiac surgeon. He sent an application to the National Heart Foundation seeking a modest sum of 377 pounds, nine shillings for relocation expenses from Minnesota to Sydney. He was granted a portion of this sum, for which he was extremely grateful, and in January 1972, my family returned to Australia.

A work colleague, Professor Michael O'Rourke, said that back then Dad's appointment at St Vincent's was a breath of fresh air. The hospital already had a strong and highly innovative surgical department, but the workload was heavy. Harry, especially, was tiring. Dad, whose stamina always amazed me, was in his mid thirties and worked easily and productively, forging a reputation as a highly skilled and competent surgeon, and one who demonstrated excellent judgement. Michael O'Rourke was the same age as Dad and watched his career progress in parallel with his own. He recalls, 'In the '70s, we had the biggest and busiest coronary care ward in Australia; initially the only unit with mechanical heart assistance, and we were receiving referrals of the sickest patients from all over New South Wales. Victor relished problems, and I took many to him.'

In his memoirs, *The Heart of a Surgeon*, published shortly after he died in 1987, Harry Windsor wrote about his impressions of his protégé:

From the outset his intelligence, dexterity and confidence were apparent, so Mark and I were delighted when he told us he would like to specialise in cardiac surgery. By this time training was easier to obtain and Victor enjoyed the best available in the world at the Mayo Clinic, the advantages of which have been obvious ever since . . . Victor revealed himself as a genial, open person, with a tendency to

think aloud and bare his soul. Shyness was not part
of his makeup. Short, with a round face,
bespectacled, correct and impeccably neat in tailored
suits, jackets and button-down shirts, his dressing
reflected the meticulousness of his surgical technique.

Dad worked with Harry Windsor and Mark Shanahan
for ten years. Harry and Mark had optimised their
experience by assisting each other in every operation,
be it large or small, and Dad willingly joined in this
tradition. He and Mark worked together literally thousands of times, on one side of the operating table or the
other—sometimes the surgeon, sometimes the assistant. Through this arrangement a bond of trust and
cooperation developed between the men which was
not only of great benefit surgically, but it also
cemented their friendship outside the hospital.

Any operation, and heart operations in particular in
those early days, could suddenly go wrong, as only a
surgeon knows. Mark Shanahan recalled that to have
the support of a colleague like Victor or Harry at those
times was a great help. He says, 'All three of us were
grateful for that support often enough, which is why
we sometimes compared ourselves to the three musketeers of fictional fame.'

My Uncle Harry and Uncle Mark, as I knew them
then, were an important part of my family's life. To me,
Harry was an imposing, white-haired figure. I was a
little afraid of him but he endeared himself to me by

describing a useful way of saving chewing gum—by popping it behind your ear so that you could savour it again whenever you felt the urge. He would always check my ears to see if I'd taken his advice!

I didn't realise until much later that Dad did not have many very close friends in his life. But these two men were family. Also, they had a special 'connection' when they worked together. Harry tried to explain this in his book:

> It was a pleasure, until sickness intervened, to continue assisting Mark Shanahan and Victor Chang in the operating room. There, in an atmosphere of quiet and calm they work . . . uncommonly well. They both teach by practising their sure technique, which observant residents and postgraduates, both Australian and foreign, have absorbed. We have had many tough struggles together; we have had arguments and problems, which never lasted long . . .

Dad worked well with Mark and Harry, but later in his career, when he had developed a strong private practice, he moved from the position of staff surgeon to become a cardiac consultant at the hospital. Then towards the end of his career he set up his own consulting rooms at St Vincent's medical clinic.

The operation I attended when I was fourteen years old would be the first of many I'd watch Dad perform. For that first valve replacement operation, Dad had prepared me by briefing me in the car as we drove to St Vincent's. He explained that he would be replacing a heart valve—it doesn't sound as glamorous as, say, a heart transplant, but I didn't really care, as long as I was up close.

The heart was exposed, lying there in a pool of blood, cradled in a smooth sac of fibrous tissue which holds it firmly in place. It looked like a reddish-brown ball with the lower end somewhat pointed and the blood vessels on its surface were surrounded by some yellow fatty tissue. I thought about the symbol for the heart; it didn't look like that at all.

In spite of the heart's mystical reputation, it is amazingly simple. It's merely a mass of specialised muscle arranged into two thin-walled chambers (the atria), which receive and momentarily store blood; and two high-pressure, thick-walled chambers (the ventricles), which pump the blood around the body and create blood pressure.

I could see the heart still moving, twitching, but Dad warned me that soon the patient would be on heart–lung, and the beating, rocking movement would come to a halt. Circulation would then be the responsibility of the machine and Dad would open the heart and empty it of blood. I asked about the valve inside and why it had to be replaced. He explained the answer in the simplest way possible: there is a series of valves in every human heart; each valve is comprised of two (mitral) or three (tricuspid) 'leaflets'. They are like little parachutes because they are pliable and have multiple strings of fibrous tissue attached inside the ventricles to keep them in place. Under pressure they billow into a dome-like shape and press against each other to prevent any leakage. Considering these leaflets flap back and forth at least 70 times per minute, non-stop for a lifetime, it is not surprising that constant wear and tear or disease might mean the valve needs to be replaced. Sometimes, the thin transparent leaflets become thickened and out of shape, sticking together; sometimes they become weak and stretch. Either way there is an excessive load on the heart muscle, which ultimately leads to heart failure.

Dad explained that the surgeon's task is to reverse this process by replacing the old diseased or damaged valve with a new one. This time it's an aortic valve replacement—the replacement valve has been taken from a pig's heart. Sometimes valves are taken from cattle or from other humans, or they can be prosthetic. That is, engineered from metals, plastic or combined materials.

I remembered the clear glass pyramid that once sat on my desk at home; suspended inside the prism was a prosthetic valve with two metal flaps. I used it as a paperweight and I often studied it. During the operation I wondered how the theatre staff know what's what with the clutter of catheters placed inside the heart; there are plastic tubes everywhere and many hands holding them carefully in place. What would happen if I tripped over one? A sickening noise distracted me from my ruminations, a suction line, rather like the one my dentist uses, spluttered in an effort to keep the area free of blood.

Through the small opening, Dad manipulated his

instruments—forceps, scissors, needle and suture holders. They were remarkably long, like metal chopsticks. Now he had my full attention. He wasn't wearing his usual specs, I thought to myself, they must be special operating glasses. He looked intent, hunched over the table, a position that I predicted would later give him back problems. He attached the new valve using a series of single stitches called sutures; there appeared to be about twenty of them. Each suture was sewn into the patient's tissue and spread out in a circular fashion around the opening until all were in place. It looked terribly complicated. If the assistants got the sutures out of order or tangled, it would be disastrous. The sutures were then placed with needles into the artificial valve. The valve, like my paperweight, had a soft cushion, or sewing ring, around the perimeter for this purpose.

I didn't know how long I'd been standing there, but my legs were starting to get sore. How does he do it for hours on end, every day? I thought. He must be fit just from standing.

Dad guided the valve down along the sutures into the body and carefully checked it for positioning before each suture was tied, four or five knots in each one, to ensure it was secure. Because of the small opening, he could only snug each knot into place with a single extended finger, and initially he felt rather than saw that it was correct. The technique was incredible to watch. It was the first time I realised how dexterous he was. His hands were moving so fast, I could hardly make out exactly what he was doing. It's called a one-handed knot, and Dad's finger was rapidly hooking the suture over itself in one movement, with just one finger. There must have been about twenty sutures and he was knotting each one about five times, so by the end of this knotting frenzy he had created 100 knots with 100 fast finger movements, all in a few minutes!

That's when he asked me, 'See how easy it is, Ness. You can do that, can't you?' It's a moment I will never forget; it made such an impression on me that I would repeat this story when I gave my eulogy, many years later, at St Mary's Cathedral. It struck me that this man really was a surgeon, with nimble fingers and a well-organised mind.

He cut the sutures close to the knots. There was a lot more to check before the cavity could be closed, for instance, all the air from the heart chambers needed to be carefully evacuated. But I was too tired to stay and watch the closing up. I wanted to get home to tell Mum and my brothers about the miracle I'd just witnessed and how proud I was to have been there.

As a university student I visited my dad regularly in his consulting rooms after my day on campus. During my visits he would proudly show off his rooms and all the equipment. He had cupboards full of gifts from grateful patients which he'd try to pass on to me. Many of them were unopened because he was so busy operating and trying to catch up on his paperwork. Some of my last conversations with my father took place in his consulting rooms, where he was able to relax and enjoy what were, unknown to him, his final years of practice.

2

Many homes

Do those important first years of our lives shape our personalities for the rest of it? Perhaps for my father, they did. He was born in a dangerous and uncertain time, as war clouds gathered over the Pacific area. In the first ten years of his life, he would move from his 'home' five times. My grandfather, Aubrey, spent World War Two moving his family from place to place, each time fleeing from Japan's invading forces to preserve their lives and strive for a high standard of living. This meant my father and his brother and sister had an unsettled childhood.

From China's glittering capital, Shanghai, where my father was born, the Changs moved south to the 'fragrant port' of Hong Kong, thence to Mandalay, east again to Chungking via the Burma Road and finally back to Hong Kong. After the war ended in 1945, the family lived in relative peace for three years. Then, when my father was twelve, his mother was struck down with breast cancer. In 1948 she left her children in Hong Kong and set out for Australia, in the hope of finding a cure for her pain. Dad never saw her again. After some years of mourning, he was sent to Australia with his little sister on a steamship. It would be ten years before he next saw his father and 25 years before he returned to his beloved China.

The history of the Chang family in Australia stretched back further than I ever expected. In piecing together the story of my father's life, I waded through family documents, letters and photographs, and one of my first discoveries was that Dad's family background in Australia had its origins in Tamworth, New South Wales. My great-grandfather on Dad's side arrived in Sydney in the late 1880s, lured over by a friend who had told him there was money to be made growing tobacco on Australian soil. He ended up in Tamworth.

In 1985, six years before my father died, the Tamworth Historical Society wrote to him, asking him to provide an account of his life. The society had discovered that Dad's paternal grandparents were Chinese immigrants who had lived there. He was happy to oblige and sent them a brief outline of his background.

Like any family history, there was success in places and tragedy, too. I found a story of Australia, China, Hong Kong and Burma, and a family's constant flight from invasion and war.

Soon after his mother died from cancer in 1948,

fifteen-year-old Victor Chang was sent to live in Australia, a move that dramatically changed the course of his life. It was in this country that Dad took his first steps towards fulfilling his aim to become a doctor.

Details of my great-grandfather Peter Chung (Chang) Fung's life are scarce. He was born in Canton (Guangzhou), China, in 1869. A greengrocer by trade, he arrived in Australia at the turn of last century and lived in Tamworth. He ran a small shop in Peel Street, probably a general store, and went on to become a founding member of the Wing On Company in Campbell Street, Sydney.

Peter Chung Fung met and married Isa Ken You, who was also from Canton. After their wedding in Sydney in 1904, the young couple moved to Marius Street, Tamworth, where they had four sons: Leslie, Aubrey, Charlie and Stanley. They also had two daughters: Evelyn and Eileen. Sadly, Isa Ken You died shortly after World War One, a victim of the Spanish influenza brought home by troops returning from the war.

Peter remarried and his new wife, Flora Lau, gave him two more daughters, Ellen and Beatrice (Fung). Beatrice, the youngest daughter from Peter's second marriage, would be affectionately known by her future nephew, Victor, as *Luk Gow Jeh*, the Cantonese term for 'Aunt number six on father's side'.

I have always known Beatrice as Aunty Fung. She

looked after Victor like a mother and ultimately had a great influence on his life. I have had the pleasure of learning most of the facts and stories about my father's childhood and teenage years from long talks with Sixth Aunt, who is now 76, and her husband, my Uncle Reg.

Aubrey Chung Fung, my grandfather, was No. 2 (son), the second of Peter's sons. Born in Tamworth in 1910, he changed his name to Aubrey Chang when he was old enough. The Chinese tradition of placing the surname before the given name was confusing for many people in the West. It is still quite common for Chinese people to simplify their names to avoid confusion.

Aubrey married my grandmother, May Lee, in 1935. Four years younger than Aubrey, May Lee was from the neighbouring town of Narrabri. Her father, Thomas Pan Kee, ran Pan Kee's, a well-known general store in the heart of Narrabri. Thomas and his wife, Choy See, had married in Canton in 1899 and, like Peter Chung Fung, had migrated to Australia in search of opportunity and perhaps a life of prosperity.

Both Dad's parents were Australian-born Chinese. Their families, along with thousands of other Chinese, moved to Australia in the late nineteenth century. Eventually, both families would leave Australia and move back to the East. Peter Chung Fung recognised that he would be able to make a better living in China so he took the family to Shanghai, where he eventually helped establish the Wing On Department Store. May's family went to Hong Kong.

Aubrey Chang, who gained a university education in

Shanghai, was five foot eight with black hair and bespectacled brown eyes. He was considered handsome by Chinese standards, a distinguished man with a serious look about him—a typically conservative Chinese gentleman with old-fashioned values. He described himself on his passport as a 'merchant', an exporter of goods. In fact, he had a half partnership in a thermosflask factory in China.

Old photographs of May Lee show her as a petite, classical Chinese beauty, very elegant and immaculately dressed. Aubrey's and May's parents were acquaintances, but their children didn't meet until the early 1930s. They first met in Shanghai, most probably at a family gathering, while May was on holiday from Hong Kong. In a brief history of my father's childhood—a long letter Aubrey wrote at the request of Dad's close friend Dr Saw Huat Seong in 1991—he said that his and May's courtship lasted a couple of years. Then, on 27 November 1935, they were married. Their marriage certificate states that the marriage took place in the Church of St Paul 'according to the rites and ceremonies of the Church of England' at Glenealy in Hong Kong. May Lee was 21 years old at the time; Aubrey was 25.

The newlyweds settled in Shanghai on the Great Western Road, an extension of Bubbling Well Road, which continues on to the famous Nanking Road. They lived there until war would force them to flee.

Almost a year after Aubrey and May were married, May gave birth to their first son, Victor Peter Chang.

There was great excitement in the Chang household. Aubrey could not believe his luck—a son! He called his home shortly after the birth, his voice quivering with excitement down the phone. He announced, 'It's a boy, it's a boy!' That was all he said. The baby was named Jen Qien (the Cantonese pronunciation is 'Yam Him'), which means 'holder of humbleness or modesty'.

May recorded the date and time of his birth in her passport as 21 November 1936, 11.35 am. No birth certificate exists. The hospital was on the Great Western Road, where the family lived; notes scribbled by May translate it as 'Dr Sun's Hospital' but the exact name is unknown.

As the family grew to know and love little Victor— the English name he was given—Sixth Aunt gave him the nickname 'Ah Dih', meaning 'little boy'. She called my father Ah Dih for the rest of his life.

As an adult, my father never knew the actual date of his birthday. Some official documents state that he was born on 25 November 1936, but Sixth Aunt is adamant that it fell on 21 November. Chinese characters written by May seem to authenticate the 21st as the 'true' date. So our family celebrated his birthday somewhere between or on either of these days. I used to wonder whether he knew and chose not to tell us so that we'd celebrate twice each year!

In July 1937, eight months after Dad was born, the Sino-Japanese war broke out in China. This war converged with World War Two, ending in the Japanese occupation of many Chinese cities. Fighting spread rapidly and, in 1938, major cities on China's east coast were invaded and occupied. Shanghai, where my Dad's family lived, was abruptly invaded. Along with thousands of others, they were forced to flee from their home. As an Australian citizen, Aubrey held a British passport, which meant his family was officially requested to leave the settlement and evacuate to Hong Kong. Victor and May were put aboard a British destroyer and transferred out at sea to a waiting coastal steamship bound for Hong Kong. Aubrey remained in China to wind up his business affairs and joined them two months later. The sea trip was uncomfortable and rough, especially with a newborn. One night, Ah Dih was tossed out of his bunk as the ship hit rough waters in the China Sea.

Dad spent the next three years in Kowloon, Hong Kong. He was a cute little boy and thoroughly spoilt by his adoring aunts. Some of the surviving black and white photographs taken atop their Hong Kong apartment reveal an adorable, happy child with lively brown eyes, much like his father's, which betrayed a hint of cheekiness. In one photo his characteristic slight tilt of the head and bashful, knowing smile, probably recorded when Dad was three years old, captured a side of his personality and a facial expression that would remain with him in his adult life. The photographs also portrayed his jet-black hair and large pair of ears, of which he doesn't appear to be self-conscious. The Chinese believe that large ears mean longevity, hence the

Chinese sitting Buddha with long, dangling ears, so perhaps he never thought that his ears were a reason for embarrassment.

In 1938 Victor's sister, Frances, was born. A year later Aubrey's employer required him to move to Singapore, where he stayed, separated from his family, for almost a year. In late 1939, as tension between countries grew once more into ominous proportions, Aubrey sent for the family to leave Hong Kong and meet him in Burma (Myanmar). He went ahead to the capital, Mandalay (Rangoon), and the family followed him soon afterwards. May travelled with her two babies and an elderly servant/nanny named Ah Mui, who had been hired in Hong Kong to look after Victor and Frances.

Aubrey, who by this time was working to help the Chinese troops in the war effort, could continue to earn a healthy income for the family in Burma. 'Victor,' he said, 'by this time was showing . . . signs of being hyperactive, constantly up and moving around and fiddling with whatever things he could lay his hands on.' In September 1940, May's third child, Anthony, was born. He was barely four months old before the family was forced to move again.

After the first raid by Japanese bombers over Rangoon, the Changs, along with thousands of others, fled Burma. It was 1941. They travelled east along the Burma Road to Yunnan in south-western China, where they stayed for several months. On the Burma Road the family lost all their personal possessions, including birth certificates and photographs, when their transport lorry rolled over a steep precipice.

They then ventured further north to Chungking, China's wartime capital in the province of Sichuan, and it was here that they settled until the end of the war.

Our family would know little of the detail of these events if it weren't for the memoirs of Sixth Aunt. In the 22 years I shared with my father, he very rarely recounted these years spent in the care of his beloved mother. They were probably some of the happiest years of his childhood. Perhaps it was the lack of evidence, lost in the ravine, that contributed to his silence about this time in his life.

Although these were war years, uncertain and turbulent for the family, Dad was provided for in the best way possible. He started his schooling in Chungking, quickly becoming fluent in the Sichuan dialect and making friends. Aubrey's letter says that it was at this time that his son Victor:

> showed signs of weakness for living things but also [proved] himself to be a failure in trading and business, [for] which I was to tease him for many years afterwards. One of his schoolmates had a silkworm that was spinning a cocoon. He was so interested in the worm that he took a gold pocketwatch from a drawer and exchanged it for the worm. He also exchanged a bicycle pump for a cricket. He had never shown signs of being athletic but continued to show signs of intelligence.

The years in Chungking were colourless, with everyone hoping for an end to the war. This came in the spring of 1945. With Japanese surrender imminent the United States was assisting China, but Chungking was already in the midst of civil war. With the city crippled by a weak economy and low morale among the troops, Aubrey grew fearful. That year, May and the children flew back to Hong Kong. Again, Aubrey's business meant he needed to travel alone and several months later he joined the family. As far as Aubrey was concerned, and contrary to my belief, in these years his children were able to 'imbibe in their infantile minds, subconsciously, the sudden uprooting from one place to another which I think served them well in later years'.

Once in Hong Kong, the family lived in Cumberland Road, in the affluent district of Kowloon-Tong. Victor continued to have a close and loving relationship with his mother. In fact, my mother recalls that Dad would often reflect on this period of his life and talk about it to her. He felt he was his mother's favourite child.

Life for the Chang family finally began to settle down. Now permanently established in their new home, the children were happy. Dad was enrolled at Kowloon-Tong Primary School, not far from his house, studying Cantonese, among other subjects. Soon, all traces of the Sichuan dialect he'd learnt had faded.

The peace the family found in ordinary life was soon shattered by the devastating discovery that May Lee had a lump in her breast. It was found to be malignant carcinoma, or breast cancer. Towards the end of 1947, Sixth Aunt went to live with May and Aubrey to care for the family. By early 1948, May was in the advanced stages of cancer.

My father would tell this story to my mother many times during his life. By the time he had reached the age of twelve, he recalled, his mother seemed always to be in bed, sick. He would walk down to a little apothecary at the end of Cumberland Road and buy healing herbs for her. Then he would cook the special herbs himself and climb onto her bed to administer the medicine. Aubrey describes my father watching the disease spreading and witnessing her agony with no one coming to her aid.

Of course in those days there was little that could be done by orthodox medicine. Aubrey heard of a man in Sydney called Mr Braun, who had claimed success with cancer patients. Apparently he had quite a large following so, as a last resort, Aubrey took May to Australia in February 1948 to see this man. Despite these desperate attempts to help her, May Lee passed away on 7 April 1948 in a caravan in Ashfield, suffering intense pain until the moment of her death.

Aubrey organised to transport his wife's remains back to Hong Kong and she arrived there on 27 May. This day would have been her thirty-fourth birthday. The man who claimed the cure for cancer, it was later discovered, did not even have medical qualifications. According to Sixth Aunt, he was exposed all over the national newspapers as a quack. But this was too late for May, a woman who was gentle and kind and a popular, well-liked member of the extended family.

Dad said that for three years, the family wore the customary black armbands to signify a time of mourning; the children's friends were not allowed to enter the house and they were forbidden to go to the cinema. I imagine that, for the children, especially my father, who was so close to his mother and who was old enough to comprehend the implications of her premature death, this was the greatest tragedy of their lives. The memory of his mother's death haunted Dad but it certainly didn't dampen his spirits. In fact, as time would tell, this event would motivate him to achieve much greatness in his life.

Dad lived in Hong Kong with his family until 1951, long enough to hear Mao Zedong proclaim the establishment of the People's Republic of China. Aubrey was still travelling constantly for his business. Sixth Aunt raised the children with Ah Mui until the end of 1950, when she left Hong Kong for Australia.

She was devoted to the children and tried to instill in them traditional Chinese values. She remembered their birthdays and she made sure they did their homework. Naturally, she grew close to the three children and her fondest memories are often just the simple family scenes that still play in her mind. This is one of her recollections:

Ah Dih grew up full of mischief. I remember once arriving home from work to find him on top of the roof fixing an aerial with the frightened Ah Mui looking on. I implored him, unsuccessfully, to come down. Other evenings I arrived to find Ah Mui chasing the three of them who were riding their bicycles to escape from having their baths. But they always behaved when I told them to!

There are many stories like this one that portray Dad as a mischievous little boy and not much changed as the years went by. My favourite anecdote is one that Dad himself told Mum. It involves a small Victor left alone in his father's house, in which there was a piano. Intrigued by the mechanics of the thing, he decided to dismantle it and lay each piece out neatly on the floor. When this part of the operation was complete, he found that he couldn't remember how to restore the instrument to its original state. He was duly punished by his father.

Here were the beginnings of a mind inquisitive about the way things worked, essential for his future profession. Much to the chagrin of my father, his first son, my brother Matthew, would inherit the same fascination with the dismantling and putting together of valuable objects.

In 1950, aged thirteen, Dad travelled by bus, ferry and bus to his high school, St Paul's Boys College in Bonham Road, Hong Kong. Newly built, St Paul's was run by a retired army major from the UK who was notorious for his quick temper. It was at St Paul's that Victor met Peter Lee and they soon became firm friends. Peter, an architect now living in Sydney, recalls the first time he met Dad:

> We noticed each other one day when he was reading a model aeroplane magazine. I was deep into aeromodelling at that stage. We went to a quiet corner to exchange knowledge—not on school books! Then we invited each other to visit our homes to see each other's aeroplanes. We both had three to four planes constructed, also model jet cars that ran on solid fuel. Every time I brought a model car to school, Victor had a bigger one! They gave out smelly smoke and made so much noise that the headmaster finally banned us from bringing them to school.

Peter and Dad were so obsessed by their modelmaking hobby that they took handicraft lessons. In these lessons they were allowed to construct whatever took their fancy, so they built aeroplanes. While other boys arrived at school clutching books for their lessons, Dad would turn up with a great big plane under his arm. This obsession obviously meant that his grades weren't spectacular.

Of Dad's schooling years, Aubrey said that he made friends, mostly with boys who had similar interests to him. He always passed his exams without any trouble, but he was never at the top of the list. As early as 1946, Aubrey noticed that his nine-year-old son was meticulous, building toys in fine detail then exchanging them for something else that took his interest. Aubrey realised he wouldn't be a smart merchant, 'but it showed that

Victor would put together all things in very fine detail and do a very good job at it. One of his teachers in later years remarked that he could have become an excellent engineer after seeing his handiwork.'

Each Wednesday afternoon, the young Victor's last class was religion, which meant attendance at church. Dad and Peter would always sit on the last bench, sliding down as far as they could to avoid being seen by the supervising teacher. During the sermon, they would take out a cellophane tube of salted beans and munch on them. The boys were eventually caught and kept back to write out their lines, 500 times each: 'I must not eat in church.' Dad was a typical, naughty thirteen-year-old boy.

After Sixth Aunt moved to Sydney in 1950 to be closer to her friends and family, Aubrey, who described his role as 'father and mother', soon found it difficult to look after his three children. In 1949, with the Communist takeover of Hong Kong, business had slumped. Then, in 1950, the Korean War erupted. Aubrey wrote, 'Again, the uncertain years of warfare are my first concern and the children's safety from it.' He contacted his eldest brother, Les, who was living in Sydney, and explained the situation, that he was contemplating sending Victor and Frances to Australia because the political situation in Hong Kong was unstable. Aubrey asked Les and Sixth Aunt if they would act as guardians for these two children if they moved to Australia. They both agreed.

In 1951 the two eldest children were bundled onto a ship bound for Sydney, Australia.

3

Foreigner

At the age of fifteen, Dad was sent to Australia with his younger sister, Frances. The anguish he felt after his mother's death was only just beginning to subside, but he was a resilient boy who was now quite used to moving from place to place. The difference this time was that he would be going to a faraway place where he did not speak the language; neither of the children had heard English spoken before. Despite this seemingly sad situation, my grandfather noted that Dad was prepared to go and he was very enthusiastic about it. He set about booking a sea passage for himself and his sister and bought all the necessities required, leaving 'most cheerfully'. The next two years would be uncertain for Victor, who battled with the Australian vernacular and tried to find his place in this new society.

As soon as the children left the port of Hong Kong, Dad naturally assumed the role of parent. The voyage took three weeks by steamship and the trip was tough and tiring for the children. Dad described it as horrific, and Frances didn't cope well with seasickness. Both children were relieved to reach their destination, albeit scared and unsure. Uncle Les, Aubrey's elder brother, now 92 years old and still living in the same Sydney house he lived in then, went to collect the children. He remembers with affection the first words that passed between him and his nephew at Circular Quay:

> The ship docked. I went aboard wondering how I would identify them—there were many children arriving. I shouldn't have worried—they found me. I asked Victor, 'How did you find me among such a big crowd?' He replied, 'I had to find someone who looked like my father.' Very smart, I thought!

Les had strict instructions from his brother to give the children everything they needed for their education. If they wanted extras, he should use his own discretion and bills would be settled between the two brothers at the end of each month. Aubrey also mentioned to Les that Victor could be a bit of a spender.

In the future, Dad and his Uncle Les would enjoy many weekends together, tinkering with cars and going on fishing trips. Victor had an affinity with Les that he never had with Aubrey; the two of them loved one another like father and son. But Les couldn't provide a home for the children when they first arrived, because he was living with his wife and children with his in-laws and there was no room. They were billeted to Les's youngest brother, Charlie Chang, and his wife, Maggie, in Eighth Avenue, Campsie. They already had two small children of their own, Dicky and Danny. Both Maggie and Charlie have now passed away.

Frances and my father were enrolled at non-academic local schools near their new home. This wasn't ideal and seemed to go against Aubrey's original intention to provide his children with the best education possible.

Dad, at fifteen years old, was a gangly, excitable young man. He still had his big ears and although braces had corrected his buckteeth, he had a distinctive gap between his two front teeth. This added more character to an already comical face. Later in life, when he would appear before the media and attend press conferences on a regular basis, vanity got the better of him and he had orthodontic treatment to close the gap.

Dad was placed in the lowest class for his grade, one reserved for migrants who could not speak English. He missed much of what was being taught in the first six months because he didn't understand the language. However, he comprehended enough to realise that he was probably the top student in his class and wondered whether there would be any challenges for him at this school. He discussed this with Uncle Les, who decided to enrol him at another school.

Thirteen-year-old Frances was a shy young girl in first form at a local school in Canterbury when Pearl Porter (now Pearl Hansen) met and befriended her. Pearl remembers Frances as 'the only Chinese girl in the school, extremely pretty, a delicate and dainty girl'. The two girls were faithful friends. Pearl, a pretty, fair-skinned girl with curly hair and a dazzling smile, was introduced to Victor during one of her many visits to Charlie Chang's house in Campsie. Her friend, Marjorie Burnett, was there to witness the encounter and described it to me:

> My first memory of Victor was when my friend
> Pearl and I went to visit . . . Frances in her home.
> Suddenly all these people [Victor's cousins] came
> streaming out of the house, seemingly all talking at
> once. Vic followed them out and sat on the side
> fence, an amused expression on his face. I watched
> him watching us. He was wearing blue jeans and a
> white T-shirt . . . They were the first Chinese I had
> met.

Despite this new friendship, Frances was gloomy and depressed. Desperately homesick, she cried every night, distracting Victor from his studies. She told him she wanted to return home. She was so insistent that in 1953 her father, Aubrey, sent for her. Charlie Chang and family, accompanied by Pearl, went to the airport to say goodbye. After the sad farewells Dad asked Pearl whether she'd received his little note. She hadn't. He explained that he'd surreptitiously slipped a note into her schoolbag when she was visiting Frances one day. The note asked, 'Would you please be my friend too?'

Dad and Pearl, both fifteen years old, established a strong, loyal friendship. They saw one another often over the next eight years and Pearl kept a detailed diary of that time. My first contact with her was after she sent a long letter to my family following my father's death. I visited her in 1991 and she gave me precious letters and photographs that document much of Dad's life from his arrival in Australia to his early university years.

Stories like this one about Dad slipping a note into Pearl's bag gave me a real insight into his personality. I'm quite sure he thought that anything was possible. And he was certainly willing to put his humility on the line and ask for Pearl's friendship. As a foreigner arriving without any formal education in the English language, he seemed to assimilate very well. He already had relatives in Australia which would have been a help, but it is more likely that his gregarious nature helped him more than he ever knew. He used his resourcefulness to make friends and live a relatively normal life.

Mum once asked Dad whether he'd ever been the victim, in Australia or England, of a racist comment. He replied, 'No, I haven't and I refuse to look for them.' He wouldn't allow the possibility to exist—I don't think it would have crossed his mind that he was different. But I do know of one episode, again related by Pearl, that Dad may have forgotten. This is Pearl's version of events:

My mother adored Victor but my father, who'd been a warrant officer in the army, was outraged that I was spending time with a Chinese boy. On one memorable day he ordered him from the house! Shortly after, Victor came to visit again and, since he wasn't allowed in the house, I spread a rug on the back lawn. It was evening and Victor and I were innocently chatting when my father found us and came storming out of the house to throw Victor out again. I was always terrified of my father but I bravely stood up and confronted him. It was the only time that I'd ever spoken back to him so he was shocked when I told him angrily, 'You said Victor couldn't come into the house. We're not *in* the house. Where do you expect us to go? Victor is my friend—do you understand, he's my friend!' My father backed down and Victor and I hastily left. As we walked down the street to the bus stop, Victor stopped and kissed me. He was so proud that I'd so staunchly supported him, as he knew what it had cost me to defy my father.

From 1953 to his final year in 1955, Dad was enrolled at Christian Brothers Lewisham, a school known for its academic and sporting achievements. One of the brothers offered to give Dad English lessons privately every day after school. This was a godsend for him and he never forgot the brother's kindness. In his early days at St Vincent's, he would constantly remark to Sister Bernice how marvellous it was to have had this opportunity.

At Charlie Chang's home, both the family and my father were finding it difficult to adjust to one another, with Dad and his two younger cousins arguing much of the time. After one year Dad left Charlie and Maggie to live in a dormitory with other foreigners on student visas. Then, at the end of 1954, he moved to Punchbowl to live with Sixth Aunt, her husband Reg, and their two young sons, Matthew and Lawrence. In the care of this kind and loving couple, Dad settled down and experienced a stable family life for his last and most important year of school.

Dad loved Reg and Sixth Aunt as any child loves their natural parents, and when he was older he continued to visit them and include them in all aspects of his life. Just like 'real' parents, they exhorted him to study. Uncle Reg told him it was his last chance to make something of his life. Thirty years later Dad confessed to Reg that he never forgot the fear he felt after he had this talk with his uncle.

Even though he was always disciplined in study, Dad's grades at school were still not remarkable—his scores in the final year were two As and four Bs. Peter Lee, Dad's old primary school chum from Hong Kong days, was living in Australia by this time. He remembers that Dad studied very hard, putting in long hours for his Leaving Certificate. During winter nights he wrapped himself up with blankets to burn the midnight oil and he made sure that Peter stayed up to revise with him. Funnily enough, for my own HSC exams, Dad encouraged me to nap until evening, then wake up late at night and study into the early hours of the morning. At night he'd creep downstairs with vanilla milk and Nodoze to keep me awake. I never told Mum as it was our secret. He told me he had a photographic memory (unlike mine) so it was easy for him to read his books only a couple of times and remember the whole lot.

Despite being diligent with his studies, he, like all young students needed time-out to break the tedium. The boys made sure their breaks were not wasted. Dad still had the naughty streak he was born with, as this story from Peter Lee shows. I do not wonder at the strife my two young brothers and I got up to when we were children.

Victor's aunt was out and we were target-practising with his pea air rifle. A pigeon flew into the backyard and we quietly shot it—guess what we had for lunch! Pigeon and vegetable soup prepared by us. We found out it had a ring band around its leg and that it was the next-door neighbour's pride and joy, so we had to hurriedly put the feathers and bones in a council bin.

Dad's all-consuming passion for modelmaking was still very much alive and he directed much of his energy towards the pursuit of perfecting the planes, cars, rockets and boats he had under construction. He passed his skills and knowledge of this art form to his two young cousins, Dicky and Danny, whom he loved teaching despite their arguing. There was no doubt he preferred his hobby over getting good grades at school.

Brother Healey, Principal of the Christian Brothers College in Lewisham in 1955, said that the young Victor was a quiet, well-behaved and courteous boy who 'was more interested in science . . . than English . . . He was not regarded as one of our brightest students.'

In the meantime, Dad, ever the obedient son, kept Aubrey abreast of what was happening in his life. He communicated with his father once a week, writing letters in which he reported his every move, explaining everything he did and why he did it. Strangely, Aubrey didn't visit his son in Australia for ten years.

In 1955, Dad passed his Leaving Certificate. Sixth Aunt told me that when Dad left the exam hall at Lewisham, Brother Healey told him, 'You won't make it, Chang.' In spite of this or because of it, he did pass; the Leaving Certificate exam results were published when he was on holiday and he celebrated his pass by drinking a large quantity of his uncle's scotch. This is when he discovered that he had inherited the Chang trait of being allergic to alcohol. Technically, it may not be called an allergy, but it seems that many Chinese people suffer from alcohol intolerance whereby their system is unable to metabolise it—they just don't have the enzyme for it. The manifestation of this intolerance, for Dad, was a mean-looking rash, together with welts and a big red face. My brothers and I are cursed with the same intolerance. Dad never forgot it and I can only recall one occasion when I saw him with an alcoholic beverage. I was very young and he was standing by an old English dresser at home laughing with

some guests. He was holding a glass of white wine—
maybe he was minding it for it for a friend.

Lewisham's 1956 Annual Yearbook summarised
each student in the 1955 leaving class. Dad's description reads: 'Victor conquered language difficulty to
obtain matriculation; gave us all an example of persis-
tence: now doing Medicine at the University.' The
accompanying photo of my father shows a serious-
looking young man staring out from the page wearing
(uncharacteristic) round spectacles.

His plans to become a doctor were running
smoothly so far.

4

Student doctor

I have always admired people who know what their true calling is in life—whether they are born with a dream that they feel driven to fulfil, or whether they acquire it slowly over a period of years. To be able to say to yourself, 'This is what I want to do and this is how I'm going to make a difference,' is rare and wonderful. Dad decided at the age of twelve that he would devote his life to the defeat of suffering, a noble mission statement that may sound trite, but he was one of those lucky people. In 1956 he took the first step towards making it happen as he entered the grounds of Sydney University to study medicine. From this time on, my impression is that life became a little easier. His English still needed some more polishing, but he became a more focused and confident young man.

I am often asked why Dad chose to study medicine. There's no better way to explain it than to say that medicine chose the man and not the other way around.

Peter Lee said that at the age of fourteen Dad was 'a quiet person with deep thoughts and a strong conviction that he had a destiny to fulfil'. I have learnt that there was one overwhelming explanation for his drive and several contributing factors to his subsequent success. Witnessing the slow and painful death of his mother, suffering from cancer when she was 33 years old, was the most significant event of his young life and the primary influence on his decision to study medicine. This tragedy, for the twelve-year-old boy, was so indelibly imprinted in his psyche that it imbued him with strength and determination, and guided him towards making medicine his world. Perhaps he already knew this as he administered Chinese herbs to his dying mother; perhaps he had a taste of what it is to cure the ill, and this made him feel good about himself and gave him a sense of purpose. Aubrey wrote: 'These awful moments of time etched in his mind the suffering of human beings from sickness, and later in his life when asked why he choose medicine as a profession his answer was to help people by relieving them from their pain in illness.'

Sister Bernice, who was Mother Rectress at St Vincent's Hospital for many decades, first met Dad in 1958 when he was a third-year medical student. Now a senior sister working for the St Vincent's Clinic Foundation, she remembers what this shy student said to her about his motivation to study medicine.

I asked him what made him choose medicine and come all the way out to Australia to study. He said,

'When my mother died, I was very upset. I thought and thought about it. Finally I came to the conclusion that if I was a doctor I might be able to help other mothers and fathers get well, because I knew what it felt like to lose my own mother.'

Another factor that propelled him towards the field of medicine, specifically surgery, was his insatiable urge to use his hands—to dismantle and repair. His hands were his gift, special instruments with which he was endowed and which he used to exercise his sharp eye and nimble fingers. He had a natural passion and genuine talent for intricate work. What better place to apply these skills than within the field of medicine, as a surgeon?

Uncle Les explained what he observed in his young nephew: 'He was so dexterous with his hands . . . he used to do fine, intricate carvings. He had excellent concentration, too, at times . . . I thought he had the qualities required to make an excellent surgeon or a scientist . . . '

Dad's personality traits also led him to work as a surgeon. Patience, perseverance and compassion—characteristics he demonstrated throughout his life—stood him in good stead for the field of medicine. Human life and the emotions that go with it are fragile and need an understanding and empathetic personality, together with the doctor's ability to communicate and instil trust. I don't think my father, at the age of nineteen, would have had quite the same insight into his own talent and motivations, as I examine the reasons in retrospect, but he would have known that no other profession would do for him.

It seemed that the pursuit of his medical degree was the balm needed to settle Dad into a pattern of study that would make Sixth Aunt happy. Her urging continued, but it was at a different level now. Dad was aware of the necessity to study hard, but Sixth Aunt brought to his attention that each year he passed brought with it the opportunity of a government scholarship. She appealed to his sense of competition, a key aspect of his personality that existed despite his modest demeanour. As Mum has said, 'he was competitive, he knew what he wanted, and he knew he would get what he wanted, but he did it in a most gentlemanly fashion'.

Sixth Aunt's encouragement again produced results and at the end of first-year medicine, and for each year after that, Victor won the prestigious Commonwealth of Australia Scholarship, enabling him to fund his studies.

It was in Dad's second year at university that he met Michael Allam. Michael remembers those times:

I first met Victor in 1957 in second-year medicine at the University of Sydney because we were alphabetically close. We got to know each other while working on 'the bodies' in the dissecting room. We kept in touch, but not closely. For one thing he took a year off to do a

Bachelor of Science (Med) in pharmacology when he quite impressed his tutor.

In late December 1957, the end of his second year of medicine, Dad wrote several letters to Pearl Porter. He was holidaying at a farm in Victoria owned by Uncle Reg's brother, Archie Young. He went there with some of his university friends, picked apricots and turned brown in the summer sun. I enjoyed reading one particular letter, reproduced here in part, because it shows a relaxed and happy young student, a side of my father appreciating time off, which would be a rarity as he grew older. It also presents him as a quietly confident man despite his worrying about recent exams—he needn't have worried because that year he won the Prosectorship Prize in Anatomy. Dad wrote:

I didn't do so well in the exams, not as good as I wanted to . . . thanks for asking. I wish I [was] confident enough to say that I've passed. But as there are so many students in the year I just couldn't say that at this stage. It was supposed that the results will be in the papers on 30 December but the date is only a supposition, it could be a few days after that. Don't be too surprised if you don't see my name in it. I was very disappointed and depressed after the anatomy exam, the exam was very easy and I've been working very hard on this subject hoping to get a good pass when the exam comes. I had a good chance to come near the top in the class but gave it away by making some *@#!! silly mistakes and bye-bye to a distinction pass! By the way how's your mother's hand going . . .

VC

PS If I have my 21st birthday party when I come back to Sydney, do you think you can come along?

Pearl did attend Dad's twenty-first birthday party—on 1 March 1958 at his Uncle Les's house in Seaforth. The majority of the twenty or so guests there were Chinese. She says:

I searched for weeks for a suitable present. I wanted something valuable that [Victor] could proudly keep. He didn't drink or smoke. I didn't want to buy clothing that he'd discard in a few years, so I finally bought a beautiful Royal Doulton statue of a mare and foal from Prouds. It was quite magnificent, but then I agonised over its suitability for a young man of 21. I didn't even know if he liked horses.

The party was lovely. I don't remember there being any other Australian people present but I clearly recall an exceedingly beautiful young Chinese girl named Neena, I think, and I remember thinking that Victor should be dating her. I was collected from home, treated most graciously by everyone and escorted back again by Victor and his uncle in the family car. I still hadn't given Victor his gift and the longer I put it off the more embarrassed I became. On arriving home at 4 am . . . as I got out of the car,

I pushed it into his hands. I never did find out if he liked horses but when my twenty-first birthday came around he gave me a lovely pair of bookends—horses!

Two years later, in March 1960, Dad entered Wesley College on the campus of Sydney University. This was to be his fifth year of medicine, except that he interrupted his course to undertake a year of medical research work. Through this work he gained a Bachelor of Science (Med) in pharmacology. In his curriculum vitae, Dad described his research as 'into the transmitter substances at sympathetic nerve endings'. His lecturer was Michael Rand, a distinguished pharmacologist with a special interest in smooth muscle work. A preparation used by Rand was the rat cremaster muscle, which had to be dissected free from its nerve before starting an experiment. Dad had shown extreme agility in dissecting the nerve, so much so that his dissection had acquired a place, mounted in a jar, with his name on it in one of the labs.

I received a condolence letter from one of his fellow students from that time, Helen Boyd, who gave me an insight into Dad as a young medical student at work and at play:

Victor and I [were] research students together in the year that he did his B.Sc. (Med) with Mike Rand in the Pharmacology Department at Sydney Uni. in 1960. We worked closely together for a year, sometimes 7 days a week; in a close-knit team that became like a family. Our desks and equipment were all in one large space. It was exciting, that year of discovery. Victor did his first live animal surgery then and his incredible talent was already obvious. I remember one day when he and I were operating on a cat together, he said 'I'm going to be a famous heart surgeon, you know!' He said it with humour, as was his way . . . and with quiet resolution, which was also his way. And he was right.

In that year we worked together we had such fun too—I knitted Victor jumpers and he bought the phonogram into the lab, and then amongst the desks and operating tables, he taught us the cha-cha. The four of us went skiing together—seeing snow for the first time. We delighted in it and I have a lovely photo of Victor about to launch another snowball at me, having just got me full face with one. It captures his warm and wicked grin and his mischievousness and vitality—it is how I'll remember him.

Dad published his first four articles in medical journals as a result of his research and Professor Rand urged him to consider a career in surgery. Rand also suggested that Dad undertake a PhD but he confided in Sixth Aunt that this would delay his goal of obtaining his medical degree. So he declined. 'I've got my B.Sc. (Medical) degree . . . ' he wrote to Pearl in November 1960, 'and had passed with First Class Honours and now I'm back at the hospital finishing my clinical training. I should be a qualified doctor at the end of

1962. Right now I've got some exams to complete before getting into fifth year medicine.'

I had many conversations with Dad about his university years. Most of them consisted of me probing him with questions about whether he made any friends—was he a nerd? Was he still in contact with anyone from his university days? He told me how hard he studied and insisted to me that he made no friends, that he would sequester himself away at the bottom of Fisher Library all week and over the weekend, too, with all the other conscientious Chinese students. It seems that he may have misinformed me, judging from this excerpt from the Sydney University Review Book (Medicine, 1960–61).

Entering College and a B.Sc. (Med.) course in 1960, Victor, with examiners well under control, was already acquainted with the vices of University life, being in proud possession of one well-worn, well-warmed Renault 750 and one sweet, young, blonde ballet student. College 'balls' afforded him the ideal opportunity to organise very big parties and also to conduct cha-cha classes for friends not 'with-it'.

Yet, after his year of pharmacology research (assisted by numbers of unsuspecting cats and rabbits), we were not surprised to hear of the First Class Honours awarded him. Medicine V then accorded a status rise to the VW class and apparently inspiration sufficient for Victor to accumulate another flying pass with the result that he is now boarding within St Vincent's, taking with him our best wishes for his final year of Medicine and for his life as a 'Doctor'.

In Dad's academic records from 1956 to his finishing year, I was surprised to see that his scores were mostly passes, peppered with credits in subjects such as botany, zoology, biochemistry, medical ethics and surgery. He graduated with his Bachelor of Medicine in 1962, finishing his sixth year of study at Sydney University with a credit in surgery. In a photo on his graduation day on 1 January 1963, he looks very pleased with himself!

After ten years, he was reunited with his father, who made the trip to Sydney specifically for the ceremony. Aubrey said, 'Much to my delight, I found that he'd matured more, was most alert to all questions put to him and told me that he'd like to go abroad for next studies after internment in Sydney. He had planned his future way ahead of his graduation, with care and confidence of what he would become and what stature he would achieve in life.'

The Senior Yearbook in 1962 stated that, 'One thing he has been noted for is his speed in answering questions in tutorials before we had time even to think of the significance of the question. His academic record is a sure guide to the success we're all sure he'll gain in the future.'

5

Personality and passions

Of course I only ever knew my father through the eyes of a daughter and often that means that the view is somewhat distorted. In my research, I have stumbled across some fascinating stories and anecdotes recounted by friends and family that show a side of my father I wasn't aware of. I have recorded some of these insights to describe, as much as I can, his personality and his passions.

There seems to be a very large group of people—both men and women—who gravitated towards Dad in his lifetime. He built up a wide circle of acquaintances over the years. Many said they found him to be a very attractive person.

Everyone I interviewed for this book, when asked about their impressions of my father, expressed the same sentiments: the Victor Chang they encountered had a warm, bright personality; he was humble but charismatic; and his caring attitude, especially towards patients, shone through. He inspired people to achieve more than they thought possible.

As for friendship, Mark Shanahan gave me an insight into his friendship with Dad when he told me this very personal story of his own family tragedy. He has kindly let me tell this story here. Mark described Dad as a colleague whose skill, judgement, compassion, generosity and achievements he greatly admired, but he also considered Dad to be his best friend whom he 'loved as one might love a younger brother whose star is always bright and forever on the rise'.

In early 1978, my brother, Timothy, two years my senior and my lifelong hero, died suddenly and without any warning from a cerebral haemorrhage. He was dead but his body lived on. At the time of our second heart-transplant procedure in 1974, our unit had committed itself to this concept of brain death, which facilitated organ transplantation by allowing organs to be removed in a healthy state while the circulation was still intact. Not everyone, however, was comfortable with this concept, and the nursing staff caring for Tim at a peripheral hospital were not prepared to terminate his life-support systems to enable the planned removal of his kidneys, as had been approved by his family. As I was on the staff of that hospital I could choose to do so myself.

But I needed support, too, and I turned to Victor for advice and reassurance. Without hesitation he volunteered to be with me whenever this needed to take place. And so it was with Victor's hand on my shoulder that I was able to throw that switch to the 'off' position, in the quiet and eerie dimness of the ward close to midnight. Our families did not know what we were about to do and as we left to return to our homes Victor put his arm around my shoulders and simply said, 'I'm sorry Mark, but from now on let me be your brother.' And so it was for the next thirteen years until his life also ended tragically and without warning.

Dr Saw Huat Seong, who also considers his relationship with Dad to have been as close as two brothers might be, is a cardiac surgeon practising in Singapore. He describes his very first meeting with Dad.

Victor egged me along to the operating room, chatting with me like we had years of being apart to catch up; he scrubbed and gowned and in no time flat he had me facing him across the operating table, working together on an elderly patient with a heart block. That was how I came to meet Victor and that was the beginning of more than a decade of blossoming friendship and camaraderie. Victor . . . was an affable person, easy to get along with and someone who, without much effort, put you at ease right away. And right to his dying day, I had no reason to change my opinion.

When I asked Dad's brother, Anthony, to tell me something about growing up with my father he said, 'I spent little time with Victor because he was sent to Australia shortly after our mother's death. I really know very little about him other than that he was a very famous doctor and I am very proud of his achievement and success.' I was saddened when I read this summary, as it confirmed my impression that the family had been irrevocably torn apart by the death of May so early in the children's lives.

Dad didn't have a close relationship with either of his siblings; Frances moved back to Hong Kong and later moved to Canada, where she would eventually marry and have three sons. After Aubrey sent the two eldest children to Australia, he sent the youngest, Anthony, to the United States. Tony trained there as a pharmacist and became a US citizen, also marrying and having three sons. He now lives in Hong Kong.

As the years went by, the three children rarely had contact with one another and today, my own family is not in contact with them, so regretfully I cannot paint a picture of my father as a brother, even in my own mind.

But what of Dad as a son? I know his relationship with his mother was very good, both he and Sixth Aunt have told me so. Sometimes I wonder whether he would have become a doctor if May hadn't died. My father never spoke of his relationship with my grand-father. Much of what I have learnt is through my own mother, but that isn't enough to complete the picture.

To me, Aubrey was a stern, conservative old man who was not partial to Westerners and he did not approve of women voicing their opinion openly. He told me so when I was about thirteen years old, saying that I was far too outspoken for a little girl and that I should learn to hold my tongue.

Even though there were several years of silence between Aubrey and my father, with Aubrey refusing to communicate because of Dad's marriage to Mum (who was not of Chinese extraction), Dad still had great respect for his father. He was an obedient son who tried in every way possible to please his father, except when it came to love and marriage, as Aubrey elucidated in the long, biographical letter he wrote to Dr Saw Huat Seong after Dad's death.

Some time in 1968, Victor wrote to tell me that he'd like to get married to Ann Simmons, whom he'd met earlier, and with whom he'd like to go through in life. I have never been comfortable with mixed marriages and told him so in no uncertain terms and this probably, in his life, was the only time he had acted against my wishes. In subsequent years I observed that he probably made a choice that he could live with and I suppose after a certain time he made many attempts to make amends for his disobedience. Before this happened, he wired to say that they had their first baby and again when the second was born he sent a cable announcing its arrival.

Then, in August 1972, when father and son were back in contact, Aubrey offered the following opinion to Dad about his career choices. He said, 'I note you're now getting used to the backward ways of Australia. In a few years' time, while there might be other miracles being developed around the world, you could still be working in the same rut.' This says more about the 'old man', as Dad referred to him, and their relationship, than any analysis could.

Despite 'the silent years', when the 'old man' cut off contact with his eldest son and our family, as my father's reputation grew in Australia and Asia, Aubrey slowly began to reconcile the relationship. Dad would have been delighted that he was 'accepted back', even if his own family was not included in Aubrey's cold embrace.

Father and son were not alike. Aubrey's hardness contrasted considerably with Dad's compassionate, gentle nature. But ultimately they overcame their personal differences, Dad by 'making amends for his disobedience', and Aubrey by finally relenting and showing that he was proud of his son's medical achievements—in his own way. In his letter, Aubrey had one last thing to add, and it was about the time Dad and he spent together.

In the following years [contact] was short and far apart but . . . was maintained by a long-distance call mostly twice a week. With the advent of the cellular phone the length of time we could converse was after his work on his way home every evening. We spent about twenty minutes speaking with each other.

The approval Dad sought from his father spilled over into other parts of his life. My father could not stand to be disliked. This was one thing that frustrated him to the point of distraction. Sister Bernice agrees:

> It was recognised by everyone, his devotion to the sick; he liked to feel that he was doing his very best for everyone, but he also liked to feel the patients liked him too. He got quite upset if they didn't. He'd say, 'I can't go home until I've gone down to see Mr X, he was not very nice to me this morning.'
> [Victor] had such wonderful human traits . . . he felt so deeply for people when they were sick and he just wanted to get them all better. It was very sad when someone didn't get better. It didn't happen often and when a patient was sharp with him or upset, he would take it in such a personal way. Most others would walk away, but he would try to make them feel better.

After Dad performed open-heart surgery on Kerry Packer, one of his first comments, made in an interview, was: 'I don't think he liked seeing me, it was a bad sign.' Coincidentally, Rosina Johnston, who worked as head nurse on the transplant team, also mentioned this side of my father:

> Some things really stick in your mind. Tuesday mornings, Victor's operating day, I had tea ready—white with one—by 8 am when you heard those very distinctive footsteps coming down the hall. The one thing Victor hated was being ignored, so if you felt he was being difficult, you had a perfect defence mechanism!

Although many of his patients became his friends, his fear of them disliking him was always a lurking dread. I have often heard that he had a wonderful bedside manner with his patients. They thought he was 'the best' and with his skills they would be all right, no matter what. Mum often joked with him that he saved all his charm for his patients and none of it for his family! And he once remarked to Michael McBride, the coordinator of the heart transplant program at St Vincent's, that a patient's total belief that he could work 'miracles' often made him feel nervous or worried. This may be so but the patient never would have known it!

After six years of overseas training at some of the most prestigious institutions in England and the US, and with at least ten years of experience, Dad was able to establish a good reputation for himself. Real 'fame', if you can call it that, only came to him in the 1980s when the first reports of his involvement in heart transplantation began to filter out. As the years progressed, his reputation and fame increased. But Dad was not always comfortable with this.

I am still approached by people who tell me how much they admired his work, how terrible it was that he was taken away from us, then they tell me how they met him. Often these people are patients and anonymous citizens who know I'm his daughter. I try to keep a low profile; it's difficult to know how to react. Always a little embarrassed, I just say 'Thanks' and walk away, when really I should say, 'Thank you so much for saying that to me, it means a lot to me that you are acknowledging his life and his work.'

When I think back to how Dad handled fame, I'm amazed he was so graceful about it. My most vivid memories are of family dinners, once a week at a Chinese restaurant. I would witness shy looks from people in the tables that surrounded ours, then the looks would turn into blatant staring, then the stare would become a dare and, before you knew it, there'd be a couple of people milling around, asking Dad, 'Are you Victor Chang?' A few giggles of embarrassment would follow and the person would go back to their table to tell everyone that, yes, it was Victor Chang. Dad never got annoyed. He handled it beautifully and was always friendly. Perhaps he enjoyed it, I don't know, or perhaps he grew so used to it that it no longer bothered him. Whatever the case, it wasn't a problem for him. And it astounded me that more often than not, the person who approached him was either a friend or relative of someone Dad had operated on last year, or ten years ago.

From all the letters my family and I received after Dad's death, some of which I have included in the last chapter of this book, most were from his grateful patients. Bill Lee, a well-known Sydney restaurateur and one of Dad's heart transplant patients, wrote that:

> Time has gone quickly. It is now ten years since Victor passed away. I can see the Victor Chang Cardiac Research Institute growing in strength, benefiting more and more people. Regularly, I meet with some of Victor's former patients. They look fit and well. We often talk about how wonderful Victor was. It seems that he had never left us. He is always alive in our hearts. Victor is not only my doctor, he is my friend.

Mark Shanahan has also said some wonderful things about my father:

> I don't believe that Victor ever sought greatness, but it came to him easily. He was without any doubt a great surgeon and a great Australian and he was also a great ambassador, revered in some other countries as much as he was in ours. His legacy continues to benefit the people of both Australia and Asia through

those whom he taught and encouraged to succeed. He was also a pioneer with great vision for the future and with the philosophy that if you could imagine something and work at it diligently enough, then it could become reality. This is an outlook common to many great people.

This is a glowing reference from Dad's teacher and friend.

Doctors' patients must be the most grateful people in the world. They must have made him feel like he was untouchable—they put so much faith in him and they told him so. He was aware of the effect of having patients who would seemingly go to the ends of the earth for him, but he felt the same way about them. I've heard heart surgeons often referred to as having 'heart surgeon's megalomania'—it's easy to understand how a surgeon would feel superhuman, after all, they are responsible for bringing people on the brink of death back to life. Mum often told me that Dad, like many of us, thought he was invincible. In an interview, he acknowledged that, 'Surgeons, by nature, are egoistic. They do not want to recognise their limitations and for that reason many of them will get into trouble. The smart surgeon will know when he can accept a patient and when he can't accept a patient, that is why my advice to many young surgeons is not to tackle anything difficult when they are starting off.'

Dad used his humour to alleviate patients' fear and tension before an operation, and often this humour is noted as one of his most defining characteristics. From his earliest years, through his student days to university and onwards, the reports are consistent. Pearl Hansen remembers that he had 'a delightful personality, full of fun with a fine sense of humour'. Here, she relates one of her experiences with Dad:

> Throughout the first three months of 1958 Victor and I saw one another almost daily. He was a firm friend, he had perfect manners and was always reliable, gentle and caring. However he was always teasing me—you would have to describe him as cheeky! I clearly remember one day at [Sixth Aunt's] house, he was showing me his microscope. I watched him take a hair from his head and he surreptitiously wiped it clean, thinking that I hadn't noticed, and put it under the microscope. Then he took one of mine, but did not wipe it, and put them side by side. He joyously pointed out to me that his was clean and mine was dirty! Later, when he was training to become a doctor he would tell me gory tales about the morgue.

Mark Shanahan also told me about an incident he thought epitomised Dad's good humour and natural-ness in a serious situation. It took place during his Royal Australasian College of Surgeons (RACS) fel-lowship examination in 1973. On being asked by an examiner to describe the operation of a scalene node biopsy, Dad, with a sparkle in his eyes and a chuckle replied, 'I don't do them—I give them to the registrar.' The examiner persisted. 'What about tracheostomy?' Dad replied, 'I don't do those either!' Exasperated, the examiner said, 'Then tell me how you teach the registrar.' Dad passed the exam and received his FRACS. Dr Saw Huat Seong commented that, 'Only Victor could get away with such an exchange.' Afterwards, the examiner, who had not met Victor before, was heard to comment, 'He's a very likable chap, isn't he?'

Recently I discovered that my father stayed in a boys hostel run by St Vincent de Paul from some time in 1959 through to early 1960, when he moved over to Wesley College. The place was called Epiphany House, and it was a Catholic hostel in Ben Boyd Road, Neutral Bay. It cost Dad twelve pounds per week, which included two meals a day. The hostel is no longer standing—in its place is a block of residential units. I have one photo taken at Epiphany, just before a party. Dad looks happy, grinning out from the back row of a large group of Asian boys.

Peter Lee, Dad's friend from their boyhood days in Hong Kong, helped him to get a place there with two young men, the Cox brothers, from Kuala Lumpur. Peter said that during that time he and Dad studied hard and played hard. Apparently there were a lot of girls living in the neighbourhood and the boys used to peer out of the French windows upstairs at the young ladies lined up at the bus stop. Dad was a great one for practical jokes and needed to avenge a trick that had been played on him. While one of the boys was standing at the window, Dad crept up behind him and pulled his pyjama pants down around his ankles, exposing the boy to an audience of girls who saw everything and screamed in horror.

As an adult, I now recognise the humour I sometimes failed to see when I was very young. I thought my father was quite mad when he insisted that tying my tooth with cotton and attaching it to a slamming front door was the least painful way of removing those small first teeth. He once filled a bowl with delicious-looking white squiggly snacks and offered me one. I happily took one and popped it in my mouth. It was humiliating for me to discover that it was foam from the big cardboard box that had held our new TV set. Do all parents play cruel tricks on their children? I wondered.

Dad's ability to dispel tension through humour was a talent he was born with and he used it in a gentle, non-sarcastic and mischievous way. Some may not consider Benny Hill to be a comedic genius but my father and I were great fans of some of his earlier work, especially his skit of a Chinaman being interviewed by a stuffy Englishman. The bucktoothed Chinaman wears a pair of thick, dark-rimmed glasses, very similar to those my father wore in his early twenties. He is trying to convey to the interviewer that the cost of an item is 'Dirty Doris'. The dialogue goes on and on until finally we understand the Chinaman to mean 'thirty dollars'. The skit mocks the Chinese accent, which is why we loved it. Jerry Lewis was another of my father's favourites, but to attempt to re-create Lewis's funniest moments here is beyond me.

Dad wasn't the joke-telling type, but he had his own repertoire of hilarious medical yarns, all told from personal experience. I will repeat his favourite story here as I think that if he were writing his own autobiography, he would definitely include it.

I can't remember exactly where this took place, but it was very early in his career; I would guess that he might have been a resident when it happened. He had not fully developed his bedside manner yet. After examining a very attractive older woman—Dad described her to me as 'shapely'—he explained whatever he needed to explain to her as she sat forward on the chair with her legs crossed. In the midst of their discussion, he noticed a very prominent mole on the lady's knee. It struck him that the mole was an unusual colour and shape—perhaps it was a malignant melanoma? Instinctively he leant forward and rubbed the mole, and as he did so, he commented to the woman that she should think about getting the mole checked. The woman jumped back, mortified at his brazenness, and as she did so, the mole disappeared from sight. The blood drained from his face as he realised in that embarrassing split second that he had not been viewing a mole at all. You see, the woman, who wasn't wearing a bra, hadn't buttoned up her blouse properly, so when she leant forward to listen to what my father was saying to her, her nipple had slipped out of a gap in the blouse. The mole Dad had seen was in fact, her nipple, which explained the odd shape and colour my father had noted and the look of horror he received when he touched it! I love this story because I know Dad, a shy little Chinese doctor in his white coat and spectacles, trying very hard with his patient, would have found this situation to be quite distressing. But he would have giggled all the same.

On the other side of the coin, I came across an interesting comment made by an old colleague of my father's, Dr Virdi, from India. He said, 'That was the enigma of Dr Victor Chang, for he was really a very private man and under the façade of good humour and frivolity, lay a sincere and thoughtful person whose intentions were difficult to judge.'

In response to this, Dr Saw Huat Seong offered me this observation: there was no enigma. To his close friends, Dad was an open book: he was a shy and generous individual—generous not only with his money but also in praise of others. Dr Saw told me how Dad once said with sincerity, 'Gee, Mark, you are so accurate,' to Mark Shanahan as he watched him operate one day. 'If a surgeon was performing well, [Victor] would be sure to compliment that surgeon,' Dr Saw says. 'Conversely, it was extremely difficult to compliment him, as he would very quickly change the subject. He would be embarrassed and amused if he had known that a tribute was made to him. In fact, had he known that his death would evoke the public outpouring it did, he would have been quite shocked and embarrassed.'

Both of these comments are accurate in their assessment of my father's character. He *was* a private person, very proud of his achievements—in private—and in public he was humble. His unique humour was often a convenient device that he used to laugh off a serious or tense situation, and compliments made him uncomfortable.

The Sydney University Senior Yearbook of 1962 says that '[Victor's] foremost interests include fishing, science fiction, clothes and calling to see a friend of his at ballet class.' Well, I believe this list has failed to mention his one 'vice' in life: cars.

Dad's obsession with cars—and it *was* an obsession—started when he began to make remote-control cars, probably around the age of ten or eleven. When he was sixteen, his Uncle Les let him go every Saturday to the car-repair garage Les owned in Double Bay to potter around with his cars and earn some pocket money repairing other people's cars. When Dad could afford his own cars, he'd take them to the garage and fix them himself. Uncle Les says that he was like one of the boys; he would work the same hours that they did and have 'smokos' with them, too. Even though he couldn't speak English very well, he still liked to include himself in the action with the mechanics. With his 'mechanical' mind, I suppose this was a fitting starting point for his hobby.

To save up for his first car, Dad worked other odd

jobs during the week with his friend Peter. The two boys cleaned rubbish from a twelve-storey apartment block in Neutral Bay and worked at a supermarket loading customers' shopping into cars. Peter told me that whenever the conveyor belt, which moved groceries from the shop to the carpark, jammed, he or Victor crawled up onto it to clear the blockage because they were the smallest.

The long list of cars Dad owned throughout his life would fill many pages so I will just present the highlights. In 1959 he briefly rode a motorbike to scoot around Sydney until he could afford his first car, an old Renault 750, which was so rusty that he and Peter spent weeks sanding it back to the metal. Later, when Dad was a registrar at St Vincent's, he upgraded it for a second-hand, five-gear Volkswagen. At some point, he also invested in a brand new white Valiant sedan, about which he was particularly chuffed.

When he moved to London in 1966, he had an MGB, a much-loved car that he often mentioned in his letters of that period. He was sad when he had to sell it—he couldn't take it with him to the US.

Guan Chong, his sponsor at the Mayo Clinic, vividly remembers his first meeting with Dad. It was a bitterly cold, sunny day in Rochester; the air was biting with a wind-chill factor of −25 degrees C. I have a photo of Mum, Dad and me, at the airport on the day of our arrival. Mum and Dad are clad in large, furry coats, and snow blanketed the roofs of houses, walkways, lawns and nature strips. Guan, his wife Margaret and their eldest daughter, Eva-Marie, arrived on our doorstep to introduce themselves. After a few minutes Dad pulled Guan aside and said, 'Guan, take me to buy a car. Otherwise my wife Ann will leave me.'

'What are you looking for, Victor?' asked Guan.

Dad replied, 'American-made, with V8 engine, must have the power, sleek and sporty if possible. I love American cars.'

It was Sunday and all the car yards were closed, but this didn't prevent Dad from jumping over the chains surrounding them. He meticulously inspected all the cars in several yards, with the wind freezing Guan's nose, face and ears. The cold was having little effect on Dad. He compared cars, their styles, upholstery, seats, discussing performance and fuel consumption. He settled for a Ford Mustang, V8 Mach I, navy blue in colour. He fell in love with this car and his voice quivered with excitement as he rattled off all of its features, as if he was describing something of exquisite beauty.

Guan soon learnt that there were three things Dad loved best in the world: cardiac surgery, his family and cars—not necessarily in that order!

Back in Sydney, the list of car purchases continues: Falcon station wagon, 1972; brown Cortina, 1973; second brown Cortina, 1974–75. I remember one particular drive we took in this car. In a family audiotape, made in 1974 to send to Mum's parents in England, Dad goes to great lengths to describe the car. He says: 'It's my second Cortina, a trade-in for the old one, new, metallic brown model with saddle upholstery, bucket seats, 2000 cc, overhead camshaft, four-cylinder engine, costing $3100.'

One day Dad was driving the Cortina, with Matthew and me in the back seat. We were travelling at a normal speed down Spit Road in Mosman, making our way towards the Spit Bridge. My brother and I started arguing—he insisted on seeing a present I had been given. He was pulling the game away from me and I was trying to stop him. Suddenly, there was a burst of fresh air from the right-hand side of the car. I saw sky-road-sky-road-sky-road, and it seemed like I was rolling up the hill, very fast, but I must have been rolling down. The underneath of a bus appeared above me; it had come to a halt at the tip of my head. And I saw Matthew, a speck in the distance, down the hill from me in the other lane. Around us, twirling on the road were Hurricane Hank, Dizzy Dan, Smart Smitty, Super Sam, Tricky Nicky and Twirling Tim— all the Battling Tops that I had been given, dancing around the two small bodies. The doors of the Cortina had not been locked properly, despite Dad asking us to do so, and we had been ejected from the car. Dad continued driving, wondering why we had suddenly stopped arguing. When he finally looked in the rear-vision mirror he saw the back seat with no kids sitting in it!

The culprit of this accident remains a bone of contention between my brother and me, but we were both guilty. We bled on the Cortina's beautiful seats all the way home. Dad pulled out the gravel from my knees with tweezers, piece by little piece, then deposited us into a Dettol bath—I can still feel the sting!

In 1974, Dad was earning a before-tax salary of $27,000. This was one of the many facts I learnt through listening to the Chang family tape recordings sent over to Mum's parents in England. Dad said that if his salary ever increased, he'd be able to afford to buy a European car.

With the arrival of Marcus, my youngest brother, in May 1974, Mum decided a station wagon would be the best option for her young family. The following year we acquired a canary-yellow Holden Kingswood station wagon. I remember this wagon well because my head was once caught in the rear electric window when Mum accidentally closed it without checking!

It was not unusual for Dad to greet a friend by asking, 'What are you driving these days?' Or he would call a friend, saying, 'Hey, there's something I want to show you—why don't you come for a test-drive in my new car!'

In the late '70s, he came home with a big red Range Rover, saying it was a popular vehicle, especially for young families, and he wanted to take us all on regular camping and fishing expeditions. Of course, he never had time. A red Mercedes-Benz station wagon eventually replaced the Range Rover and became the family car. Then there was a Mercedes 280 SL Compact, but among his most beloved cars was his light green 450 SEL 6.9.

In 1988, while taking delivery of a car being garaged on a farm in the English countryside, Marcus, Dad and I were thrilled to be able to test-drive a stunning, silver 1960s Mercedes 300SL Gullwing. We were elated to be given the chance to drive this car, very fast, down the motorway.

There were many more loves to come, both modern and antique. My favourite was a fire-engine red MG-TF, restored by Dad and his Uncle Les from its original dilapidated condition into a sparkling piece of art. Every Sunday we would drive that car around the back streets to buy the weekend papers. Dad was proud to show it off and I was happy to squash inside and be a passenger. I was very sad when he decided to sell it.

There just wasn't enough time for him to drive the cars he owned; often he and Uncle Les would spend Sunday morning fixing batteries and jump-starting cars that had been sitting around the garage for too long, waiting for Dad to show them some affection.

The cars provided a chance for Dad to get away from it all; they were his hobby and his opportunity to relax. Cars gave him an enormous amount of enjoyment. He was an avid reader of motor magazines and would study the statistics as though he were about to take an exam. He would read up on high-performance cars such as Porsches, one or two of which he eventually owned. I used to tease him, saying he must be reaching a midlife crisis as he demonstrated how his new Porsche hugged the corners of the winding roads around our home in Clontarf.

To experience this car's handling ability in a challenging forum, he enrolled in a special drive day put on by Porsche at Oran Park. He got the feel of driving fast cars on a racetrack, and then went to Eastern Creek to experience more of the same. I'm not ashamed to illustrate the naughty side of Dad's personality by telling you that every now and then, when the police stopped him for speeding, he'd just tell them he was rushing into the hospital for an emergency. Usually they'd let him go without a fine.

Dad made a handful of car-loving friends with whom he could speak the strange language of cars. One of these friends was Michael Munroe. Their first meeting, however, was not about cars. It was in 1963 at St Vincent's casualty, when Michael arrived to pick up his sister who was working there. Michael recalls how Dad approached him, asking who he was waiting for. Michael says,

> In those days, he wore heavy, black horn-rimmed glasses that went well with his unique smile. I would never have thought then that I would later meet him in 1977, and for all the years ahead, share with him his love of motor cars. I shared treasured and privileged time with him at the many auctions, concourse days, test drives and sales of Mercedes-Benz vehicles that became a business itself.

Dad and Michael spent time looking at different cars and examining their style, finish, quality of design and power, which gave Michael an insight into the private side of my father:

He loved the feel, touch and pleasure that this concept of driving gave him. Whether driving or being driven, he was able to switch off and admire the function of the car. I saw this as an extension of his profession: knowing where he was going, in complete control, and that the power was his; and giving him a 'selfish' satisfaction that he needed as a balance to his unselfish dedication to his career . . .

The solid-fuel model jet cars and P51 Mustang fighter planes that Dad built and played with as a young boy and teenager were replaced by real cars and real boats when he reached adulthood. The fighting/action story comics he loved to read when he was in Hong Kong were replaced by kung-fu movies in adulthood. Dad had a library of Chinese action movies which filled many shelves of his study. Along with car racing, tennis, boxing, old movies, daily news and violent action movies of the *Lethal Weapon* variety, Chinese martial arts movies were a true form of entertainment for him. I watched so many of them when I was younger, all in Mandarin with subtitles. Dad would point out the good fighters to me, explaining the various techniques they used to defeat their opponents. He was consumed by the movies, sitting there cracking his sunflower seeds and laughing with excitement, replaying the good bits.

*

Weekends were mostly family days. I can't recall Dad having his friends around very often, unless it was car or work related. He visited Sixth Aunt almost every weekend, never forgetting the family she provided for him when he first arrived in Australia.

Dad has been described in the past as fiercely independent and someone who abhorred government intervention in health care. This may have been so, but he rarely commented on his political persuasions in public, except to say that he wasn't political. He didn't feel it was necessary to make known his feelings on political issues, unless they were directly relevant to the work he was conducting, or if he was a spokesperson for the medical profession on a topic he felt particularly strongly about. Apparently, Dad threatened to resign in the late 1970s over a doctors' strike. His threat to resign from a public hospital was about as political as he got in the public arena.

His face first appeared in the media in 1974 when the second heart transplant had just been performed. He was described as the 'assisting surgeon to Dr Harry Windsor'. From the hundreds of articles written about him since then, it was rare to read about Dad in connection with anything other than cardiac surgery. But, as is evident from his hard-won struggle for St Vincent's to acquire the heart transplant program, he could play the game.

In the same Chang tapes mentioned earlier, Dad

talked to my grandparents about the 1974 elections. He described how the then Labor government was making noises about nationalising medicine. He felt that this was creating very severe antagonism in the medical profession and, as a result, there was bound to be fighting between the profession and the government. Dad commented that, 'They have lost a lot of votes from the medical profession and from the 98 per cent of people who are currently under the health insurance scheme.' In the tapes Dad is open about his wishes for the Liberal Party to 'come back in', but only from a medical standpoint, as he preferred this party's private-enterprise health scheme.

Every now and then I heard Dad lament about the feelings of some of his peers or colleagues. It was sometimes brought to his attention that there were some who felt he was 'too public', and others who felt he was just a 'medical entrepreneur', seeking fame and fortune from medicine. Amazingly, one such story made its way back to my father. It's important to highlight the fact that, of course, his professional life was not always a bed of roses. One day, when a hospital in Sydney was being renovated, there was a loud clanging noise—not unlike metal scaffolding crashing down. Everyone in the operating room was running about trying to investigate what had happened. One doctor, who was operating at the time, said, 'Take it easy, everyone. That's nothing more than Victor Chang dropping his loose change.'

All this provided us with material for healthy round-table dinner discussions when we children were old enough to voice our opinions, which we were encouraged to do. It dawned on me once that the development of the total implantable artificial heart might be perceived as 'unnaturally' prolonging the life of a person who might otherwise have died. I asked Dad how he felt about this. He was frightened by a vision of the future with people living with artificial hearts inside their bodies; he recognised the moral dilemma in all this, that immortality may be possible and that the total artificial heart was humankind's first small step towards it. What if all body parts could eventually be replaced, including limbs? With a continuously beating artificial heart inside the body, might there be the possibility of immortality? Our theorising finished there but this debate is still taking place.

As I write this book, I work in marketing and often wonder what contribution I am making to the world and to my community. Dad was hoping to make a doctor out of one of his children. When Marcus was born, he said, 'This one will be the doctor and follow in my footsteps.' That has not yet happened. Dad always said to me, 'You don't want to be a doctor, do you? Why would anyone want to be a doctor, look at the hours I work. I'm never home to spend time with my family!' But I knew that, in his gold-rimmed glasses, surgical cap and gown, leaning over his patients, giving them his reassuring touch and a cheeky smile, he was at home.

6

Transplanting
a heart

The world's first human-to-human heart transplant was performed in December 1967 by Dr Christiaan Barnard in Cape Town, South Africa. The patient did not survive. Other countries followed, including England, the US, Japan and Australia, where the first transplant was performed in October 1968 at St Vincent's Hospital, Sydney, on Richard Pye. The surgery team was led by pioneer heart surgeon Dr Harry Windsor and included Mark Shanahan. Tragically, Richard Pye lived for only six weeks with his new heart.

On the other side of the world, in England, Dad was watching Harry Windsor's progress with great interest. He was about to complete his second year of training as a surgical registrar at St Helier Hospital in Surrey, under the guidance of Aubrey York Mason. It would be another four years before he returned to Sydney.

Dad was inspired by what had taken place and he

was eager to find out all the details. He was particularly excited because the Australian transplant was performed by his colleagues at St Vincent's in his home town. He had never seen a transplant performed and, not wanting to be left out of the action, he asked Mark Shanahan to write to him with every little detail of the patient's progress. Mark duly did so and the letters from home became weekly news sheets.

Mark suspects it was at this time that Dad's 'unique dedication' to the success of heart transplantation began. Later, his interest would be further fuelled when he met other doctors with enthusiasm comparable to his own.

When he left St Helier he moved on to Brompton Hospital in London, which had one of the most prestigious centres for cardiac surgery in the UK at that time. At the Brompton, he met and worked with Philip Caves and Margaret Bellingham, who would each have a profound influence on the field of heart transplantation. They in turn introduced Dad to Dr Norman Shumway, a well-known American surgeon and pioneer in cardiac transplantation who performed the first adult heart transplant in the United States in January 1968.

When Dad met Norman Shumway, Norman was working at the Stanford University Medical Centre in Palo Alto, California. This was and continues to be the most eminent unit in the world for heart transplantation. Dad became a frequent visitor there.

*

By February 1972 Dad had moved back to Sydney with his new family. He replaced Mark Shanahan, who went into private practice, as the staff specialist at the St Vincent's cardiac unit. It would be another two years before Harry Windsor attempted the second Australian heart transplant. This took place in April 1974, with Dad in attendance. As with the first Australian transplant six years earlier, there was a lot of publicity surrounding the event. Both the donor's and the recipient's names were publicised, probably because the repercussions of publicly naming them—invasion of privacy for both the donor and the recipient in a traumatic time—were not fully understood in 1974. Sadly, the recipient died after 62 days due to rejection/infection complications.

It then became apparent that the facility at St Vincent's Hospital wasn't adequate for the housing and post-operative care of transplant patients. The heart transplant program was temporarily put on hold until developments in science had progressed to a point where immunosuppressive drugs were developed and their effectiveness proven. Significant funding was also needed to subsidise an ongoing, national program.

There were also some legal matters concerning transplantation that needed to be resolved, including the legal and medical definitions of 'brain death' in relation to removing the heart from the donor. This was examined in detail in 1977, when the Australian Law Reform Commission under the chairmanship of the Hon. Mr Justice Michael Kirby released its *Report* on *Human Tissue Transplants*. The report contained some draft legislation which, by 1983, became the basis for all relevant Australian legislation, preparing the path to the establishment of transplant units other than renal.

Although the performance of heart transplantation at St Vincent's was suspended, Dad continued to work towards the vision that in the future there would be a successful transplant program, specifically at St Vincent's. As luck would have it, Neville Wran, who was then Premier of New South Wales, happened to be a patient at St Vincent's Hospital. He recalls the time he first met Dad, through Sister Bernice, and their discussion about the proposed heart transplant unit.

In the middle of a particularly gloomy morning, during which I had been prodded and punctured a little more than usual, a slight tap on my door heralded Sister Mary Bernice, who was accompanied by a young gentleman who was obviously a doctor (he wore a white coat and had a stethoscope around his neck). Sister Bernice introduced the newcomer as Dr Victor Chang. It transpired that Dr Chang was a heart surgeon who was performing, with his team, advanced heart surgery at St Vincent's Hospital.

The introduction over, Dr Chang assumed the role of advocate and explained to me that Sydney should have a heart transplant unit. With restrained but obvious enthusiasm, he explained how lives would be saved; how others would be prolonged; and how

Sydney would become a centre of excellence to which the attention of the world would be drawn.

The intensity with which he spoke, the clarity with which he articulated his case, and the confidence he exuded shook me from my hospital torpor. And in no time we were engaged in an animated discussion of what a great thing such a unit would be, not only for Sydney, but for Australia, and what a great facility it would provide, not only for Australians, but for the people of the Asia-Pacific Region, to which we belong.

When Victor realised that I was ready to take the bait, he became even more animated: his eyes twinkled, his smile became more persuasive and his charisma—that is, his ability to influence or impress people—became so obviously apparent.

As a politician, as a lawyer, as a practising queen's counsel, I should have been persuaded one way or the other by the weight of his argument, but in this instance, at least at the beginning, I was influenced by the charm and persuasion of the individual presenting the argument, rather than the argument itself. By the time he had finished, the facts and circumstances supporting the argument were incontrovertible and my immediate response was to the effect that Sydney should not spend a second longer than was necessary to get a heart transplant unit, and that when I was well enough, and back in my office, I would do something about it.

I was duly discharged from hospital and resumed

my duties in the Office of Premier. At the same time I either forgot or put on the backburner my previously unquenchable desire to have a heart transplant unit, and I went about other affairs of state.

Dad probably didn't foresee that it would take almost ten years before the heart transplant program would be up and running again. In the meantime, there were important developments in science—such as the improvement of methods to assess the rejection process and, more importantly, the development of effective immunosupressive drugs.

I remember how excited Dad was one evening when he arrived home. He rushed in and announced that Cyclosporin A was ready for use; it was going to change the face of heart transplantation. But there were hurdles. The federal government would intervene and a minor drama would unfold that would see St Vincent's lose the right to set up the program, then miraculously get it back. These events weren't well publicised at the time and Dad played an important part in them.

To understand how the events unfolded we must go back to 1982 when the National Health and Medical Research Council (NHMRC) set up a working party to investigate whether a heart transplant program was necessary in Australia. The council's report, which was released to the government in June 1982, recommended that a program *was* necessary and gave five major reasons for its recommendation.

First, based on overseas experience, at least twenty patients per year would meet the criteria for heart transplant in Australia. Secondly, it was obvious from the literature available at the time that results from a responsible and properly planned program were excellent and, with the use of Cyclosporin A as an immunosuppressive drug (first used in 1979–80), results would improve further. The third reason was that cardiology units and cardiac surgical units in Australia were of the highest international standard, therefore skills necessary were readily available. Also available were necessary skills and expertise to support a heart transplant program, for example, pathology, immunology, nursing and so on. These skills were already demonstrated by excellent results in renal transplant programs. Fourthly, sending twenty patients per year overseas for heart transplant was not considered to be a solution, as the financial and social costs would be enormous. And, finally, every cardiologist the working party spoke with told of sad and terrible experiences with young adult patients, for whom every form of medical and surgical therapy had been unsuccessful, leaving only heart transplant as treatment for their illness.

It was therefore recommended that a unit be set up in Australia. It would be based initially in one hospital, preferably with an existing renal transplant program, and it would be in either Sydney or Melbourne. Existing heart surgical units in hospitals around Australia that fell within the above guidelines were invited to make a submission to the government. As with overseas programs, it was required that the establishment of a heart transplant unit would not interfere with normal, routine cardiac surgery, both in time and funding. Surgeons were expected to work for the transplant program without remuneration for the extra workload they would be taking on.

The St Vincent's submission was sent in 1983. Staff were confident that they would be granted the privilege of starting the program, but Laurie Brereton, the new state Minister for Health, announced that the unit would be established at Sydney's Royal Prince Alfred Hospital. The news astonished and disappointed everyone at St Vincent's. Mum told me that Dad was in his car on his way home when he heard the announcement on the radio. Of course, he was upset. He raced home and the phone calls started. They continued into the early hours of the morning. One of the people he called was the Premier, Neville Wran, who recounts here what took place after he first heard of the announcement.

The news of the minister's recommendation hit St Vincent's like a thunderbolt and it was not long before I intervened to have the whole issue of where the unit should be located the subject of an objective inquiry. Luckily for me—and of course St Vincent's—the inquiry determined that the appropriate place to locate the heart transplant unit was at St Vincent's.

Since Australia's leading heart surgeon, Dr Victor Chang, was at St Vincent's, few could argue with this finding. So . . . many months and many millions of dollars later, Australia had its first heart transplant unit—a trail-blazing medical development which put Sydney in the spotlight of medical practice and research, and went on to save many lives.

Shortly after the inquiry, Laurie Brereton overturned his decision, stating that Royal Prince Alfred was unable to guarantee the necessary requirements, and that the establishment of a transplant unit there would impinge upon routine cardiac surgery. In December 1983 the then federal and state Health ministers jointly announced that the program would now be instituted at St Vincent's Hospital. Both federal and state governments committed a further $100,000 each to the program for its first year of operation. It was also announced that the program was to be reviewed by the NHMRC after one year. That took place, and in September 1985 ongoing funding was provided by the New South Wales and the federal governments.

There is one more part to this story. It concerns an anonymous donation that was given to St Vincent's shortly before the announcement was made. This is how my father described the events to Sixth Aunt. A generous seven-figure sum was needed to start the unit and Dad had recently performed a bypass on an Indonesian businessman who was recuperating after the operation. The businessman was very grateful and indicated to Dad that he would like to make a donation to St Vincent's. Dad thanked him and, because he expected the man would make a five-figure donation—quite a 'normal' amount from a very grateful patient—he thought no more of it. When he called in on the man the next day to check his progress, the man stated again that he wanted to give a donation, but this time he named his figure: US$250,000, which at that time equated to around half a million Australian dollars. Dad said he was so shocked he called Sister Bernice in to thank the man. The businessman asked whether this was enough and did they need more! Together with what they had already accumulated, plus money from the federal government, they now had the required start-up funds. Dad let the government know immediately.

The Australian public would soon become very familiar with some of the individual heart-transplant recipients and the widespread media coverage informed them about the process of transplantation. A professional heart transplant unit requires a team of doctors and specialist nurses and expensive equipment to pump the blood around the body while the heart is being transplanted. Once the transplant unit at St Vincent's was set up, the number of lives it could save was only limited by the supply of suitable donor hearts.

The procedure involves removal of the diseased heart, except for some of the tissue from the atria—the two upper chambers of the heart. Leaving this tissue in place facilitates the stitching of the new heart into position. The replacement heart is removed from the donor and preserved in a cold salt solution and temperature control is critical. During implantation it is trimmed to fit and sutured into place, making all necessary vascular connections.

Great care is taken to match patients and donors in terms of their blood type and other immunologic indicators, but the body's natural immunity needs to be suppressed to prevent transplant rejection. The patient remains on drugs that allow the body to accept the foreign organ for the rest of their life. Anticoagulants are also administered to prevent atherosclerosis (hardening of the arteries) in the transplanted heart, a problem that caused the death of many early transplant patients.

In February 1984, two months after the announcement, Dad, as Heart–Lung Transplant Unit Director and Senior Surgeon, along with the team at St Vincent's were thrust into the public eye when they performed Australia's first heart transplant since 1974. As reported in the headlines of every newspaper around the nation, Dad gave a new heart to a 39-year-old shearer from Armidale, Neville 'Peter' Apthorpe. Then, around five weeks later, he operated on perhaps the best known and most popular of all the transplant recipients, a fourteen-year-old Australian girl named Fiona Coote. Having been diagnosed with cardiomyopathy, she was literally at death's door.

In an interview, Dad said that he was reluctant to

proceed with the operation because the young girl was so ill; he didn't expect her to last more than two or three days. They also had to wait for a donor heart to become available and the chances of getting one were slim. Fiona's parents made a national appeal for a donor and the program received a number of offers. By this time Dad and the team were virtually committed to undertake the operation because of the amount of public support the Cootes received. Fiona was oblivious to all of this because she was so sick.

Dad took me into St Vincent's shortly after Fiona's operation. He told me that the girl lying in the bed was the same age as me, and that she had received a new heart. I was almost as shy as Fiona and too scared to put on a gown and mask. I opted to simply tap on the window and say hello over the intercom. Fiona described to me how she felt during this incredibly emotional time.

Dr Chang and his team assessed me to see if I would be suitable for a heart transplant and decided, 'No'. That was the logical medical decision. The team had performed their first transplant in this program only weeks before. Here I was, with all my organs in failure and on total life-support, punctured lungs and far from a good chance at survival. I was also unconscious and this wasn't just any operation. If they didn't operate I would die, but with a transplant I had the opportunity to live.

I'm indeed blessed that seventeen years ago the St

Vincent's transplant team reconsidered, said 'Yes' and accepted me on their waiting list for a transplant.

I received many visits from Victor particularly with my first transplant. He would call by the window of my room most days. His standard question to me was, 'Fi, are you happy today?' If I smiled and gave a positive response he would continue on his way. If I didn't, he would go to the trouble of gowning up and come in to see what the problem was. He may have only stayed a few minutes, but he would give his attention and listen to my concerns. On other occasions he would come and play cards with Rosina [the unit manager] and me, and let me cheat and win.

I have many fond memories, but one story I'll share is perhaps unexpected. It's of my earliest recollection of Dr Chang, which, believe it or not, was terrifying for me. I had no memory of meeting him before my operation because I was unconscious. I was from a small country town and had only seen a few Asian people in my life.

Shortly after my transplant I was lying in my critical care bed, floating in and out of the anaesthetic haze. I was ventilated and therefore unable to speak. I could hear voices calling my name and when I came to, there were five people all peering down at me. The leader was particularly inquisitive and I later knew him as Dr Chang. All these people wore surgical gowns, gloves, hats and masks. The only part of their bodies that wasn't covered was their eyes. All the people looking at me were of Asian origin. I couldn't talk and had no idea where I was, because the colour of the walls and curtains had changed. The look on my face must have been one of fright and not one of gratitude for staying up half the night to perform my operation and save my life.

Fiona endeared herself to the Australian public and, in part, because of this she helped promote a positive attitude to transplantation and balanced media coverage. This was an aspect of heart transplantation that Dr Windsor hadn't been prepared for when he performed his first two transplants in 1968 and 1974. Unfortunately, he received many letters of ridicule.

Dad learnt a lesson from his experience and anticipated the intense media interest the first heart transplants would generate. He wrote to all radio station managers and newspaper editors to ask that they treat each of the cases with dignity and sensitivity when they reported the news. He reminded them that for each new heart that became available, there was a family somewhere making a difficult decision about whether to switch off life support for their brain-dead relative. So, for the joy experienced when a new heart and a new life was given to a transplant patient, an equally tragic grieving process was being experienced by the donor family. In dealing with both written and electronic media, Dad was always cautious. He would ask to see draft copies of articles before they went to print, and, where possible, he liked to be shown footage of a documentary on the unit before it went to air. Of course, this was not always possible, but he was concerned about any misrepresentation that may harm the community support for donation, which would in turn affect transplantation.

In the early years of the unit's work, there was enormous interest surrounding each transplant performed. St Vincent's Hospital also had an experienced media and PR person, Mrs Trish Burns, who would monitor stories on each case. The media reported the events in a positive and careful manner, contributing to the ongoing success of the heart transplants. As it turned out, the interest of the public and the media would go on for many years and still exists today.

It's fascinating to conceive of human beings receiving a different heart from the one they were born with—a heart from another human being. The fear that a patient feels before open-heart surgery cannot be understood by anyone who has not had first-hand experience. I went to Bill Lee to ask him what his feelings were, how he found out that he needed a new heart, and how he coped with the long wait for a donor heart. This is his story.

I dragged my feet slowly along a dark corridor with the seemingly endless stairs at the old St Vincent's Hospital. Finally, I reached Dr Victor Chang's consulting room and dropped down on a chair in front of his desk. I was having difficulty breathing and puffing like an old sick bull. My heart was pumping furiously and I could hardly say a word. Victor reached out his hand and gave me a firm handshake. He said, 'Geez, I haven't seen you for a long time. How are you?' I had to take a deep breath before answering him. 'I don't know but I'm feeling very sick.'

After a little casual chat, Victor leant over to check my neck and felt my pulse for the very first time. I looked at his face. He was wearing a pair of gold-framed glasses and appeared very serious. In a gentle tone, he said, 'Bill, I have already studied your doctor's referral. You have a serious problem with your heart. We can't waste any time and you must admit yourself in the hospital for a check-up immediately.'

I felt stunned and very afraid. I asked, 'What's wrong with me?' His face expressed concern and he replied, 'The problem looks serious so we have to check it out. If it is what I suspect, you may need a heart transplant.'

His words hit me hard. I could feel a chilling sensation going down my spine and my whole body turned cold. 'Have I come to the end of the road?' I asked. In a calm comforting voice he replied, 'No, Bill. Nowadays, heart-transplant operations are very successful. I think we can fix your problem provided the program accepts you. Besides, you are still young. You are going to make it.' When I heard those reassuring words spoken with such confidence, I looked at his calm expression and all my doubts disappeared. I knew Victor would do the best for me.

The next day, in the early spring of 1985, I was admitted into St Vincent's Private Hospital for a thorough and detailed check-up over a few days. Victor would not allow me to leave the hospital throughout this period. A week later he told me I had been accepted for the program and must wait in the hospital for an available heart. I knew that if I did not get a heart transplant I would not survive. My condition deteriorated rapidly and I was getting sicker by the day in the hospital. Every passing day seemed like a year. Victor came to see me every morning and night. Sometimes, he would bring along other heart-transplant recipients to comfort me and give me moral support. That was when Fiona Coote and I first met.

Finally, I was wheeled into the operating theatre. When I woke up, I was surrounded by a number of doctors and nurses. I saw a familiar face with the gold-framed glasses. He said to me, 'Bill, you look great! You have made it.' His words were soothing and I could feel his smile behind the surgical mask. After two long and difficult months—somewhat eased by the special care and efforts given by Victor, the other doctors and nurses—I was finally home.

After Peter Apthorpe's transplant, St Vincent's was ready to hire a cardiac transplant coordinator. Part of

the job required a knowledge of sensitive issues surrounding transplantation. Michael McBride took on
the role and described to me how it all came about.

Michael had been working in the Open Heart
Surgery Unit at St Vincent's Hospital, Melbourne, and
moved to Sydney in 1984. She had sent a letter of introduction, along with her CV, to St Vincent's and Royal
Prince Alfred hospitals. She heard nothing from St Vincent's, but she did hear back from RPA, and they
eventually offered her a position. However, days before
she accepted, she received a call from Dad, telling her
that he'd just come across her letter. He persuaded her to
go to St Vincent's the next day so that he could show her
around the Heart–Lung Transplant Unit (HLTU)—
before she made a final commitment to RPA.

He was offering a job in a unit that was only just being
established—they had performed the one transplant on
Peter Apthorpe. Her proposed 'office' was not much
larger than a broom cupboard, with a chair, table, filing
cabinet, an old typewriter and a phone 'on the way'.

Such were his skills in 'selling' a position that didn't
really exist, I felt it would be exciting and challenging
to take on this position as 'Australia's first recipient
transplant coordinator', to use Victor's words! Also, I
found the opportunity of working with Victor very
difficult to resist, as he had already inspired me with
his enthusiasm for the program. His vision for the
future was to make the HLTU 'a centre of excellence'.

Michael also described Dad's feelings about the donor families. She said he always showed the compassionate side of his nature when considering donors and their families. He would comment on how grateful he felt that people could be so generous in their willingness to become a donor and his sadness at a death, and expressed his further gratitude and sympathy for the families who agreed to donation at a time of great tragedy.

He told Michael that because her job indirectly involved dealing with the death of donors and the grief of their families, she was not to allow herself to become immune to the sadness. Michael assured him that this would not possibly happen. Dad also commented that no matter how skilled he might be at transplantation, without community support for organ donation and the generosity of donors and their families, he would not be able to use those skills. He said he felt very humble in comparison to their act of donation.

I hope that these sentiments reached the families of donors. Shortly after Dad's death, I received a condolence letter telling me so, from the parents of a young boy.

> There has been much mention of the recipients of the organs but we write to you as the parents of a donor, Grant Cameron . . . Our 16-year-old son Grant . . . was placed on life support and on the 1st of November the team came and took his organs. We did not see Dr Chang but we believe he was there.

We made the decision to give our son donor status because of Dr Chang's work and the death of a friend from kidney failure.

We saw Dr Chang speak on TV about the people who make the decision to donate their loved ones' organs. He showed the compassion he felt for families like ours who have to make such a decision at such a traumatic time. It helps to know he felt for us and appreciated our feelings. His comment that 'there is no greater gift' touched us very deeply. It has helped to know that our son's death has allowed others to live.

Rita and Bob Cameron, Duffy, ACT

Since that first heart transplant in 1984, there have been 585 heart transplants performed at St Vincent's, including those my father performed. The success of heart transplant at the HLTU was as good as the best internationally. Dad's next challenge was to expand the program to heart–lung transplants, which he achieved with government approval and appropriate funding.

He performed the first heart–lung transplant in 1986. Then he invited me and my friend, Sha-mayne Chan, to attend another at the end of that year. I have a picture of us after we'd gowned up that evening. Before we went into surgery we were bright-eyed and excited. During the operation, Dad asked us to stand next to him so we could view and touch the recipient's old lungs, diseased from asbestos poisoning. They were sitting in a kidney-shaped dish. Sha-mayne recalled the scene with great clarity.

> I found it amazing that even though [Victor] was obviously performing something very important that required all his concentration, he was still able to remember that we were there and tell us what was going on and ask us if we could see properly, etc. And his sense of humour—I remember him showing us the patient's lungs . . . which were grey from asbestosis. He told us that was what was going to happen to us if we kept smoking! And that our lungs should be nice and pink like the donor lungs and heart which had just arrived.

There have not been any great advances in heart transplantation over the past ten years. The operative technique has changed very little. The number of transplants has actually plateaued, and it may have decreased slightly, due to the fact that donors have become more difficult to find and patients have been treated in other ways. There have, however, been significant advances in lung transplantation. The first lung-only transplant was carried out in 1990 and the first double-lung transplant took place in 1991, after Dad had died. St Vincent's now performs more lung transplants than heart transplants.

Today, there are five heart–lung transplant units Australia-wide—in every state except South Australia.

This is an amazing achievement for this country, one that I am proud to say that Dad and the team at St Vincent's Hospital helped to forge.

7

Just a father

'What's wrong, Ness? Why are you upset?' Dad is leaning over my bed. He looks concerned. I'm six years old.

'I don't want to be Chinese, I don't want to have Chinese eyes, I get teased at school and I hate Chinese food.' Dad can't help himself, and his smile is the same as always: amused and crooked. He chuckles, and I think to myself how his laugh is like Mutley's, the cheeky dog character from the cartoons I watch; it's sort of a laugh mixed with a wheeze, head down, eyes crinkled.

'One day when you are older and more mature, you will be very proud to tell people that you are Chinese. You'll love eating Chinese food, too. I'll be very proud of you when I can hear you say that one day.'

This was a valuable lesson Dad taught me early in life: not to be ashamed of who I am or what I look like and, more importantly, to be proud of my Chinese ancestry. I wasn't even aware of my own Chinese-ness until someone at school pointed it out to me. What a shock. I felt ashamed and I wanted to hide it so no one would notice. It took a long time, about another eight years, for me to feel proud of the part of me that was Chinese. I went to Dad and told him that I was now proud to be Chinese and that I loved Chinese food.

This experience also taught me that Dad believed he was, first and foremost, a Chinese man living in Australia. He said as much in interviews, like this snippet I found among his papers.

I feel very comfortable working in Australia . . . I have never really felt any prejudice or felt disadvantaged. I am aware, however, that it may be so because of the circle of people I work with. I have always felt that my destiny is with my own people, even though I have assimilated very well in an Anglo-Saxon community. I have not consciously gone out of my way to prove myself; at least I don't think so.

I have always felt that perhaps I am not so needed in a community of this sort, perhaps I am needed more in an Asian society and that is the reason why I chose to return to Australia after my training in Britain and the United States. I decided to go back to Australia for a number of reasons, apart from the one that my family originated there. I felt that Australia is closer to the South-East Asian region and therefore closer to my own home, but, more importantly, to

China. In a way I am glad that I did return to Australia in 1972 because since 1977 I have been able to visit China on a regular basis, sometimes twice a year.

Dad had inherited some of the old-fashioned values of his father. He was very conscious of his role in the family unit. Often he would tell me that the reason he worked so hard and spent so much time away from the family was because he was the provider. I think he felt guilty about spending all his time at work, but the fact is, he loved his work. I must say I can't remember a time in my life when I wanted for anything. Dad was a magnificent provider. Before I started earning my own keep, there was nothing in this world he wouldn't have given me if I had a good reason for needing it. I was very fortunate. Dad was simply the most generous person I have ever known.

Occasionally he'd say, 'You kids love your mother more than you love me. She has been such a good mother to you. I never had a mother to take care of me like she takes care of you.' It was true that Mum did the job of two parents, but she obviously did it so well that I never noticed that Dad wasn't there most of the time and I didn't begrudge him for the times he didn't spend with us.

One of my few regrets, trivial though it may sound, is that Dad didn't teach me to speak Chinese. He tried to send Matthew, Marcus and me to his Uncle Les's house for Saturday-morning Mandarin lessons when we were very young, but we didn't learn much. There were about ten kids in the house and we just wanted to get it over and done with so we could play with our cousins.

Dad learnt Cantonese when he was a child, but he couldn't speak a word of Mandarin until well into his forties when he started travelling to China. He needed a translator for his first two trips there; when he returned to Australia after the second trip, he was determined to speak the *po tung* (Mandarin) dialect. He used a talkback system with earphones, repeating phrases, then playing them back to himself to compare accents. He wore the contraption at home until he became proficient enough to practise with friends over the phone. He was single-minded in his determination to learn the language and during his next trip, he amazed his hosts by dispensing with the interpreter; he even gave his first speech in *po tung* dialect.

He must have thought there was hope for me when, aged sixteen, I signed up for Mandarin lessons with my friend Sha-mayne. Alas, we wasted our lessons by eating out at Chinese restaurants in Dixon Street, Sydney's Chinatown, instead. Dad would be waiting at home, looking forward to engaging us in conversation over what we'd learnt in our last lesson, which as it turned out, was very little.

Although he was very friendly and welcoming to all the friends who entered our lives, I think he may have had a special place in his heart reserved for our Chinese friends. It sounds silly, but his great affinity for all people Asian and the comfort he felt with them was quite obvious to me. Sha-mayne, a Malaysian-Chinese who came to Australia with her family, like Dad, at a young age, remembers when she first met 'her friend's father'.

> [It was] my inaugural Chang dinner, I guess that was in 1986, and I didn't find it as daunting as you had prepared me for, until your Dad asked me if I could speak Chinese. I was young, and dumb, enough to say yes and he started talking to me in Mandarin. I then said, 'Oh no, I only speak Cantonese.' He spoke a few Cantonese words to me, and I said, 'Oh, I can't speak Cantonese, just Malaysian Cantonese . . . ' At this point I realised I couldn't even speak Cantonese! I think [Victor] had a good laugh . . . his hopes of you having a Chinese-speaking friend were dashed.

Dad was keen for me to meet a 'nice Chinese boy', preferably a doctor. Although he would chuckle when he talked about it and raise his eyebrows at me as if he was serious, it made me more determined, saying, 'Dad, I will *never* marry a Chinese doctor!'

Sha-mayne remembers popping into Dad's office at St Vincent's with me. It turned out that he wanted to introduce us to a couple of young Chinese medical residents. Sha-mayne was as keen as I was. He said, 'Just wait a minute, stay for a second,' while he went to fetch the residents, but we were already on our way out the door.

Dad hoped we would embrace our Chinese heritage

more fully. He didn't realise that, for me, it was a discovery I needed to make alone.

Then there was food. The Chinese are very serious about their meals. When a Chinese person greets you, they will often ask, 'Have you eaten yet?' This is the equivalent of the Western tradition of asking, 'How are you?' Not one weekend in my childhood and early adult life went by without eating a Chinese meal with my family.

'You are too young to appreciate Chinese food,' Dad would tell me. And, 'Your mother only married me because she loves Chinese food!' Indeed, my mum, a culinary genius and foodaholic, wistfully described how her first taste of sweet, succulent, steamed Chinese crab, dripping with light soy sauce, shallots, garlic and chilli, on a mound of fluffy hot rice, left her enraptured. She says that after that moment she never wanted to eat Western food again. It was her second Chinese meal with Dad, at the famous Lee How Fook in Soho, London.

Because of my parents' obsession with Chinese cuisine, we children felt it was unfair that we were always forced to eat this food. But we grew up to enjoy the delights of oriental gastronomy and no distance was too far to travel for a good meal. Often the family would be treated like royalty because Dad had operated on the owner or head chef. Dad would say that it was Chinese restaurants that kept him in business, often owned by highly stressed, middle-aged men who were running busy restaurants and sampling the rich food all the time—perfect candidates for a heart attack!

Marigold, Mido, China Sea, Orchid Garden, Nine Dragons, Fortuna Court, Ming Sing, Chequers Inn, Chopsticks, Regal, we frequented all of these restaurants and many more. All the waiters knew us and we knew and loved all their special dishes. From Peking duck—crisp, juicy, finely sliced duck on a paper-thin pancake with hoisin sauce—through to beggar's chicken—boneless chicken stuffed with rice, vegetables and meat—and piping-hot winter melon soup. I can't explain the taste of this savoury broth but it has the same effect as chicken soup is reputed to have on the sick: therapeutic and utterly divine.

Bill Lee, one of Dad's transplant patients, owned a chain of restaurants called Lee's Fortuna Court. We still go there to eat and Bill treats us like his own children. He'd always give Dad the large table in the corner, where we could make as much noise as we wanted to. Bill describes a visit from Dad after his transplant.

Months later, I returned to work. I saw Victor a lot less in the hospital. Instead, he came to see me in my restaurant. He would come regularly on Sunday nights with his family. He loved old traditional Chinese cooking such as double-boiled soup and salty fish with steamed, minced pork cake. One day I cooked him a dish I believed was my best dish ever:

steamed butterfly prawns with garlic sauce. He
didn't lift his chopsticks at all as he said to me,
'I hate people eating garlic. I can't eat this dish.'
Considering his line of work, I understood the
reasons immediately.

I regarded my father's dislike of garlic as a travesty—
Chinese people love garlic! But he had his reasons. He
refused to eat it because he didn't want to offend his
patients the next day. Was this worth the sacrifice? He
thought so. Mum would sneak garlic into most of our
meals at home, anyway.

Dinner was the most important meal for our family
and, like most families, I imagine, it was the one time
of day when we would exchange ideas, report on our
lives, seek opinions and argue if necessary. Mum
cooked almost every night of the week, and the meals
were often lavish affairs with plenty of visitors—
extended family, my brothers' and my friends and
visitors from overseas. We sat at a round table, the
same one we have dined at, in the same spot, for over
30 years.

Occasionally, a chef would come to dinner. Emma
Quick was one. The daughter of an old friend of my
mother's in England, she arrived at our house in 1988
at the age of nineteen. Although Emma was a chef by
profession, she needed to learn a thing or two about
Chinese food and remembers my father's reaction
when she first cooked rice for the family.

One evening I cooked some rice; seems so simple. But sitting at the round table that night, Victor piped up and said, 'Who cooked the rice?' 'Me,' I said, blushing. Victor responded, 'Well, I'll have to teach you how to cook rice properly.' I knew he didn't mean to offend me with his comment, he was simply stating that Chinese people do know how to cook rice. I still think of that evening every time I steam rice, looking for perfection. Through this mutual love of food, Victor introduced me to real Chinese cuisine.

Emma also reminded me of something my father would do every evening after dinner. I should set the scene by describing his at-home uniform. He wore old jeans and a T-shirt and, on his head, as always, his beanie. Dark blue with red and white stripes and a white pompom, he rarely took the beanie off his head, even when he slept. He wore it to keep his hair in place. It was a topic of much hilarity in the house and among my friends, who saw it as an eccentric trademark. On his feet, he wore sandals or slippers.

He always had to be doing something with his hands; if it involved food, all the better. His ritual was to sit in front of the television with a large jar of sunflower seeds. There is an art in cracking the seeds open to reveal a perfect centre, just as there is in taking the shell of a prawn in one go without damaging the flesh. Both involve precision and nimble hands, and accuracy in splitting the seed right down the middle with the teeth. If there were no sunflower seeds in the house, lychees would do—he loved both equally.

To complete the picture, when my parents finally succumbed to our desperate pleas for a dog, there was a Rhodesian ridgeback named Chammy. Dad trained her to gallop outside, collect the newspaper, bring it back to the master of the house and lay it at his slippered feet. Chammy was good at fetching the paper but she bit every member of the family, so we eventually had to send her to another family—one with no children.

Sixth Aunt remembers Dad's love of animals, especially the little Sydney silky they had when Dad was a teenager. His love of dogs is a little-known side of his nature. The silky's name was Gorgie Porgie, and Dad cared for him as if he were his own. He taught Gorgie Porge tricks—to jump through hooped arms and to sit in front of his food and not touch it until he said the magic words, 'All right, Porgie.' He also trained Porgie not to venture past the front gates onto the pavement or the road.

His success with the training of little Gorgie was not repeated with our second hound, a gorgeous beagle pup we called Lucy. No efforts to train or discipline this beautiful, stupid animal were successful, but she had lovely long, silky ears on which Dad loved to nibble. This may sound very strange, but he liked to do this. I rebuked him for it, but he never gave me a reason other than he just liked it! Perhaps her ears reminded him of his collection of cashmere jumpers, purchased in bulk on every trip to China.

I don't regard my upbringing as different from that of my friends. But then people were always approaching me to tell me they'd seen Dad on TV or in the paper. Otherwise, life was pretty normal. I could relate many, many stories, but ultimately they'd be the same kinds of experiences all families have. Victor Chang was just a father, not Chinese, not famous, not different and, at home, there was nothing unusual in his fatherhood. He wasn't there a lot of the time but since this is all I had ever known, it didn't seem wrong or unfair to me. As a child, if I ever felt cheated of his time or his love, I can't remember it. Even today, many people remind me of the hours and days Dad spent away from the family. I don't feel that this impacted greatly on my happiness as a child. I'm not sure my brothers would say the same.

Dr Saw Huat Seong's view is that Dad had few regrets in his life and any he may have had, he kept to himself. He did speak quite candidly with his friend Huat Seong about the family, saying he regretted not spending enough time with his two eldest children. He explained that we were growing up during his formative years, the years he was trying to get himself established, so he missed spending time with us as children. In speaking about me, Dad said to Dr Saw, 'A daughter will always be your daughter. She understands me and forgives me for not spending that time with her.' This is true.

I learnt from him the lessons that all children learn. He taught me how to drive, and he taught me about the birds and the bees—perhaps in a little more detail than most. I was woken up very early in the morning, Dad requesting the pleasure of my company in my parents' bedroom. I was seven. I was propped up between them both and the atmosphere was very serious. With pencils, pens and paper in hand, Dad informed that I was about to be taught about sexual reproduction. I wish I had kept the detailed diagrams he drew; they were fascinating to me and not embarrassing in the slightest. He drew the ovaries, the testicles and the journey of the female egg through the fallopian tube after fertilisation; and he explained all the bodily substances and possible difficulties that may occur. My first biology lesson took just under two hours and I understood completely and was allowed to ask as many questions as I needed to. His diagrams were excellent—he was a very good drawer. Do all children learn this way? Probably, if one of their parents is a doctor or teacher. It seemed quite normal to me.

At a very young age, perhaps when I was ten, he allowed me to drink my first beer (I detested it) and he taught me how to blow perfect smoke rings using his pipe. He must have grown tired of that because he took up cigars later, claiming that it was OK to smoke them after dinner because he didn't inhale.

Dad's hands were as steady as a rock. He'd compete with me and my brothers to see whose hands could remain the most still. He usually won, but when he

ABOVE Dad, aged two, in traditional Chinese dress standing on the roof in Hong Kong. PHOTO COURTESY OF SIXTH AUNT.

TOP RIGHT Again on the rooftop, a sweet three-year-old in overalls. PHOTO COURTESY OF SIXTH AUNT.

RIGHT Chang family portrait taken on the steps of their Cumberland Road house in Hong Kong in 1950. From left to right: Frances, Victor, Tony, May and Aubrey. PHOTO COURTESY OF SIXTH AUNT.

The three children: Dad sits in the middle of Frances and Tony, wearing an expression he would carry with him into his adult life. PHOTO COURTESY OF DR SAW HUAT SEONG.

Dad, with his favourite bicycle, arriving home from school in Hong Kong, 1951.

PHOTO COURTESY OF DR SAW HUAT SEONG.

Dad with his friend Pearl Hansen and her mother at Pearl's twenty-first birthday party in 1958. PHOTO COURTESY OF PEARL HANSEN.

This photo taken at Epiphany House in Neutral Bay in 1959, shows the boys all dressed up just before they threw a party. Dad is in the top row, second from left. PHOTO COURTESY OF PETER LEE.

Dad looking rather pleased on the day of his graduation, Bachelor of Medicine, in the sunny quadrangle at the University of Sydney, 20 January 1962.

PHOTO COURTESY OF
DR SAW HUAT SEONG.

Dad sits in the first row, second from the left, in this portrait of St Vincent's Hospital final year registrars, 1962.

ABOVE One of the few photos taken of Dad during his London days, probably around 1967, with his friend Sinha.

LEFT Mum and Dad standing outside the Surrey wedding registry only moments after they tied the knot on 20 April 1968. Mum's parents, Lois and Charles Simmons, stand behind the happy couple.

RIGHT Dad at a residents party in Minnesota with Mum (on his left) and Margaret Chong, a host family member and Guan's wife, in 1971.

BELOW Dad and me playing on the haystacks near the white cliffs of Dover in 1970. Note Dad's beanie.

With Marcus in the garden at our house in Adelaide Street, 1975.

This photo is part of a series of shots taken by my mother in the Valley of the Rocks in Devon, 1969. Dad loved this photo.

Matthew, Marcus and I at home in Adelaide Street.

Standing on the Great Wall of China in 1981, looking very relaxed.

Beijing, 1978. Dad and Harry Windsor with local Chinese doctors visiting a temple. This was Dad's first trip to China as tour leader.

Dad in Beijing again, giving one of his educational tutorials to the local doctors in 1981.

This familiar photo, taken at a press conference soon after Fiona Coote's first heart transplant in April 1984, shows the 'Three Musketeers' – Dr Harry Windsor (left), Dad and Dr Mark Shanahan.

Two friends – Dad and Dr Mark Shanahan – in the corridor of Cameron Wing, St Vincent's Hospital, following a successful operation.

The Cameron Wing operating team in the operating room.

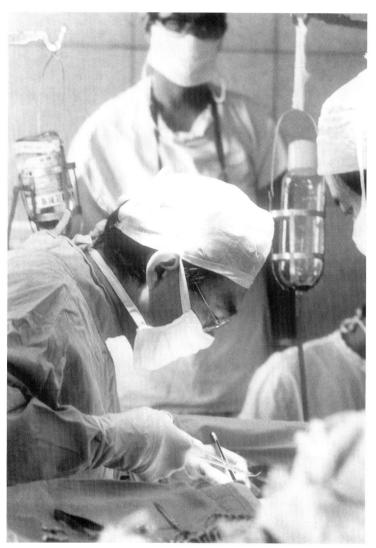

Taken at an operating theatre in China, this photograph shows Dad's intense concentration as he performs open heart surgery.

ABOVE Dad with Fiona Coote, soon after her 1984 heart transplant. Dad is examining a cheque that has been donated.

RIGHT Dad in weekend attire with his Uncle Les, about to go fishing.

A rare family photo taken around 1987. From left: me, Dad, Matthew, Mum and Marcus.

At an international symposium giving one of his many lectures.

This photo, taken in early 1991, shows Dad and Mum with Sister Bernice at a dinner function.

A happy photo taken in the University of Sydney quadrangle at my graduation in 1989. After the ceremony we went to lunch to celebrate.

didn't, we would laugh uproariously and that would teach him not to boast. Of course he was proud of his hands—he had reason to be, they saved lives. It sounds funny, but he took his hands very seriously. He didn't drink coffee or strong tea, because it would make his hands tremor and he needed them to be as steady as possible. Coke was allowed and he drank litres of it, despite its caffeine content.

Soft from years of soaping before theatre, his hands were well cared for with manicuring and moisturiser. They were fine hands, which he informed me were insured for a large sum of money. His hands, he said, were his livelihood; if anything happened to them, he could no longer provide for the family. We weren't allowed to be too rough with Dad because there was always a risk that we'd hurt his hands. Now that I think of it, this must have been the reason he wasn't the handyman he could have been. He could have worked on the house, but that would have meant possibly damaging his hands. I accepted the value of Dad's hands and tried never to squeeze too tight during our arm wrestles.

I feel I grew up in a very normal family environment, but what's normal, anyway? When you are part of a family you know each member so well that superficial things like what they look like and what their voice sounds like go unnoticed. You only know what is inside, what makes them a person and a personality.

My mum recently told me that Dad had a Chinese accent. 'What!' I exclaimed, 'No he didn't!' She insisted he did, so I watched a video of my twenty-first birthday party, playing back the part where Dad and Mum are giving a speech together. He did have an accent. I had never heard it. I guess it's the same with all families.

But I must concentrate on mine, I suppose. It's very difficult for me to speak about my experiences of Victor Chang as father and husband, despite the encouragement and faith many people have in me to be able to do so. This is because, like my father, I place great value upon the privacy of my family. I don't mean to imply that other families don't feel the same way about their personal lives, I'm sure most do, but unlike most, my family has experienced life with media intrusion—during those sunny days of the first heart transplants, and in the darkest days surrounding Dad's death. Luckily, Dad had the foresight to shelter us from media attention, always specifying before an interview started that questions about the family would not be answered.

At best, the relationship he had with the media was tenuous, but I also recognised that journalists were quite charmed by him. His coyness and youthfulness, which I have also heard described as 'boyish charm', was a quality that appealed to many people. He always seemed to come across as natural and humble when he was being interviewed for print, radio and television interviews.

He quickly learnt to handle the media and their ways. I've heard some say that Dad should have been in PR and that he enjoyed the attention. I don't believe this. He saw all the faces of the media machine. He said that the 'good' media would promote the positive side of the transplant program, informing the public and helping them to understand organ donation as well as encouraging fundraising for the program. The 'bad' media focused too much attention on him, often neglecting to give credit to the whole team. This was something of which Dad was painfully cognisant; it made him feel embarrassed and uncomfortable.

My family experienced the 'bad' media when journalists camped on our lawn, day and night, for weeks on end after his death. They knocked on our door and on those of our neighbours, greedy for a photo opportunity and emblazoning their papers with headlines and pictures that had been contorted and twisted out of all context. I understand there were stories of Dad's involvement with all sorts of sordid dealings, but I didn't expose myself to this rubbish because I knew it would make my blood boil—as it does now when I write about it. I felt the media had betrayed my father. Those who were so willing to report on the success of his life's work up to this point were now hovering over my family when we were at our most vulnerable and distraught. At the age of 22, it was a real baptism of fire for me to learn that the media had such power.

Dad was reluctant to give interviews unless absolutely necessary and, believe it or not, he declined various awards for the same reason. In 1987 he received a congratulatory letter from John Newcombe announcing that he had been selected as Australian

Achiever of that year—for outstanding contributions in the medical field, especially heart surgery. After discussions with family, colleagues and the administration of St Vincent's, he wrote and declined to accept the nomination:

> I really feel that I must give priority to the feelings of my family and my profession. (As you are aware, commercialisation is frowned upon in the medical profession.) . . . Cardiac surgery, especially cardiac transplantation, is a team effort involving doctors, nurses and paramedical staff . . . I therefore suggest that your Council consider nomination of the St Vincent's Hospital cardiothoracic team as a whole for the award.

My parents travelled regularly, often accompanied by one of the children, but when we weren't going, Mum insisted that she and Dad take separate flights—to avoid the risk of us losing both parents in a plane accident. Dad once hinted at the possibility of dying young; he thought he would meet his demise in an air crash and on at least one occasion, he offloaded himself from a delayed flight due to reports of 'mechanical difficulties'. I thought this was a rather morbid way of looking at the world.

Mum was a nervous flyer, white-knuckled and eyes shut tight at take-off and landing. Dad thought that with so much travel, the probability of an accident only grew larger. All the same, with such frequent trips, Dad became familiar with the art of crossing time zones, *always* in comfort, sleeping for most of the trip, with a constant supply of water and peanuts. On a few occasions he was disturbed and asked to help resuscitate passengers who had suffered from heart attacks or some other unfortunate episode. Other than this, up in the air, he was able to have a peaceful break from the demands of family and work.

Travel wasn't a chore for him. Apart from being away from the family for long periods, I can't remember him ever dreading it. Most of the time he was leaving for an Asian destination—back home. Having said that, he did write a letter to me in 1978, when I was nine years old, explaining how he felt.

> You know I really don't want to go away and I hate going away except when I have Mummy, you, Matt and Marcus together. That is why the last time when your mother and I went to Port Stephens, we sent for you all to join us. Unfortunately, as much as I hate being away from you all, I have to be away sometimes, to learn about new things and be a better doctor first, like you have to go to school to learn to become a better person.

Perhaps one of the small incentives for him was the shopping he loved to do, primarily because he could buy gifts for the family back home. He bought us something every time he went away, without fail. Then there were the electronic goods—he was obsessed by large televisions and gadgets. And it was even more exciting if there was a little bargaining involved; he really relished a good tussle with a salesperson, and what better place to do it than in Singapore in the early 1980s.

I learnt the subtleties (or otherwise) of bargaining at the age of twelve when Dad taught me lesson one: always pretend that you are about to walk out of the shop, this will ensure a better price. In Singapore, our usual hotel was the Mandarin on Orchard Road and it was renowned for its little café, the Chatterbox. Inside, some say, they serve the best Hainan chicken rice in Singapore. We would eat this every day when we stayed at the Mandarin and I think it was in Singapore that I really began to appreciate Chinese cuisine.

Other than the many commitments my parents had with the Asian community and at official functions, they were not a particularly social couple. I always considered my father to be antisocial; in fact, he detested socialising at functions for which he had to dress up and meet people with all the small talk he knew would be required. Most of the time this was part of his job, so he just had to grin and bear it. He preferred, when not at work, to relax at home, clean his cars, watch TV, read car magazines and visit his aunts and uncles. When we were younger, he took us out fishing, as his Uncle Les used to do with him when he was a boy.

He once bought a large motorboat, which he moored at Clontarf Marina. He didn't tell Mum because he knew she would most likely say it was a waste of money and, besides, she was prone to seasickness. To soften the blow, he had named the boat *Lady Ann*. He had come home in an extremely excited state and gathered all the family together on the verandah. He asked us to look down at the wharf, saying, 'What do you see?' We looked down to see *Lady Ann*, which we would later call 'the horrible stink boat', bobbing up and down on the water. This was a large gadget, indeed. Mum was as pleased as Dad had expected her to be, but we went on a cruise that weekend anyway. It was the first and last trip. When Mum tried out her namesake, she was soon seasick and unimpressed. Shortly afterwards, the boat was sold.

The circumstances of my parents' first meeting and subsequent courtship are probably not unusual, but I love to recount them. I have many photos of my mother, then Ann Simmons, in her twenties. She was glamorous and very sociable; a dark-haired beauty with bright green eyes and perfect teeth. Slim, sophisticated and vivacious, this English girl from Surrey had many suitors competing for her affections. She says she wasn't interested in settling down because she was too young, and she was busy making a success of the business she had just started. She had never met a Chinaman before.

At a party one evening in the summer of 1966, she felt unwell and decided to take herself off to the local hospital in Surrey, St Anthony's in Cheam. It was midnight. The doctor on call in the emergency ward that evening was Victor Chang. Ann encountered a slim man with smooth skin who looked very young—at 29 years old, five feet seven and three-quarters, he wore heavy black-rimmed glasses and a cheeky grin. Mum recounts their first meeting.

> This Chinese guy was on call that night. He was very bouncy and introduced himself: 'My name's Dr Chang and I'm on call this evening.' I told him my symptoms and he said, 'Oooh, I'd better examine you.' After the examination he diagnosed me with appendicitis, saying, 'Tomorrow morning we are going to operate on you so you'll have to stay in hospital.' I wanted to go home but he didn't allow me to.
>
> . . . I asked Victor if he'd be performing the operation. He said, 'No, Dr Aubrey York Mason will operate, but I will be assisting.'

Aubrey York Mason recalls that later that evening, Dad called him from St Anthony's saying, 'Come in quickly, please, we've just admitted a real "whizz-kid" with acute appendicitis!' The following morning Mum was duly operated on.

> While I was in recovery, the first person to visit me was Victor. Also on that ward was a friend of Victor's

and a nursing sister, Catherine Hally. Victor had obviously told her there was an interesting person in the ward because she kept coming into my room, trying to do a bit of match-making. Victor also kept visiting me and pointed out that he was fascinated by the stream of visiting friends and the flowers I was receiving from friends. Upon my departure he said, 'I'll phone you about the biopsy results.' I told him not to worry, just to send it to my doctor. But he insisted, 'No, no, in fact, I might deliver them personally.'

It was very obvious at this point that Dad was keen on Ann Simmons. She also noticed that another young doctor, a colleague named Michael Allam, was continually walking into her ward to peek on her. Dad had sent Michael to get a second opinion! Michael remembers it, too: 'I recall how enthusiastic his description was of her. Superlatives like "really beautiful" and so on bubbled out of his mouth.'

Her recovery after the operation was excellent and Mum went home to recuperate at her parents' house. She didn't think much about the doctor who was keen on her, but he was doing a lot of thinking about Ann Simmons and decided to call her a week later.

The phone rang and it was Victor Chang. He said, 'You received so many flowers when you were in hospital; I'd also like to bring you a bunch of flowers.' I reluctantly agreed and he came round with a big bunch of red roses, stayed a while and charmed my parents at the same time. I remember them raving about him, saying, 'Oh, what a lovely person, he's so bubbly,' because he *was* bubbly—really chatty and humorous.

Dad pointed out to Mum, persuasively, that he had come to England to do his FRCS (Fellowship of the Royal College of Surgeons) and that he was a new boy in England. He told her that because they both owned MG cars, they already had something in common. He added that he hadn't done any sightseeing in England, asking whether Mum could possibly show him around. She explained that she already had a boyfriend, but he just kept phoning anyway. In the end Mum felt sorry for him. She was under the impression that he was young (he didn't look 29) and was all alone in the world, so she eventually relented and took him to Brighton. They went off for the day and Dad suggested they stay for dinner. Mum's first Chinese meal was that night at the Nan King in Brighton. He wanted to teach her how to use chopsticks, which he did, but it was an ordinary meal and he insisted that he intended to take her to a real Chinese meal at a restaurant called Lee How Fook in Soho. Mum's love affair with Chinese food and Dad, too, I guess, began at that restaurant.

He started phoning again, and again I relented. He was very attentive and brought more flowers. I thought to myself, 'This guy is really persistent, maybe all Chinese are like this.' So he wore me down, he really wore me down. I didn't encourage him, but I thought maybe he was very lonely. He used to say to me, 'You are so lucky, you have your family. I miss my mother very much.' He talked a lot about his mother and how this had been the catalyst for his becoming a doctor . . . that his father was always away working . . . his mother was sick and that he was his mother's favourite child.

Many months passed. It was 1966 and the romance grew stronger. In the meantime, Dad acquired his FRCS and landed a job at St Helier Hospital. Later he would move to the famous Brompton Chest Hospital in London. But first he was summoned by his father, Aubrey, to go to Hong Kong. He suspected his father might try to match-make him with a nice Chinese girl—funny how history repeats itself. One of the ten letters he wrote to Mum in the twenty days he was in Hong Kong describes how things were going.

12/8/66

Dearest,

Your letters of the 6th and 9th came in together today and I was most excited . . . I was beginning to think that you must have forgotten me, despite my constant efforts to remind you that I'm still around.

My boss, Harry Windsor, arrived yesterday afternoon, and I've been quite busy showing him around and during a conversation he told me that if I don't wish to go to Japan, it'd be OK with him, after all he said, it won't help me to pass these exams. Further more it'll interfere with my coming back to England on the 20th. The cardiac centre in Tokyo and the superiors there are friends of his. These people are doing quite a bit of work but not successfully and certainly not first class people like the Mayo Clinic or the Baker Clinic in Houston, Texas. So it doesn't really matter after all.

As for me, I've really been a real good boy, no 'night life-ing', no 'bird watching', just plain studying and thinking of you. Now that my friend is here, he'll help me pass some time. My father is quite good, he hasn't bothered me about marriages, etc and certainly hasn't interfered with my wanting to stay home to study.

Glad to know that the B is in good hands and that you are looking after it. You are a real darling. I don't think I can find another girl just like you anywhere again! So do stay around and don't run away. I'm particularly impressed with your domestic activities what with your excellent child-rearing hips and now the development of the maternal instinct. I'd say you'll make an excellent mother. I reckon the chap who gets you as a wife will be a real lucky man?!?! All jokes aside I really think you are wonderful and I do miss you a lot, in fact very very much and oh how I wish I could see you soon.

. . . Guess I'll have to say goodbye again my

darling and I'll write again tomorrow or the day after. Cheers sweetheart and lots of love and kisses for you only.

Best wishes to the Simmonses.

Your Victor xxxx

After repeated offers of marriage from Dad and two years after they first met, Mum agreed to the union and a date was set. Not everyone was happy with the announcement.

When informed of his son's impending marriage to Ann, Aubrey warned Dad not to ruin his life 'with that white woman'. Dad also related to Mum Aubrey's threats to commit suicide if the marriage went ahead. Of course, if he made the threats, he never carried them out, and the marriage did go ahead, on 20 April 1968.

Later, after Mum had met Aubrey and came to know him she realised how surprising it was that Dad had disobeyed his father, as Aubrey himself attested to. This would be one of the very few occasions that he would do so. Aubrey didn't contact my father for three years after the wedding. This must have been very disappointing and hurtful for Dad, but being a dutiful son and prolific letter writer, he continued to correspond with 'the old man' every week during those years, never showing any animosity towards Aubrey for his silence.

Father and son were eventually reunited, in 1972,

when Mum, Dad, Matthew and I travelled from England to Sydney via Hong Kong. They kept in close contact for the rest of Dad's life, but Aubrey never accepted his grandchildren, the 'half-castes', and my mother, the 'white woman'. Similarly, Dad never criticised the old man for his treatment of his family. This was something that remained unresolved. My grandfather passed away in 1995, aged 92.

In death, Dad was just as much an enigma to Mum as he was in life. She says that she still doesn't feel she knew him completely. He had his secrets, as most of us do. Was I aware that he was engaged to an Australian ballerina before he met my mother? After much research and questioning of family members and old friends, I found that he was, but Mum had no knowledge of this when Dad was courting her. He broke off the engagement with the ballerina–nurse soon after he met my mother.

Dad's graduation picture, taken at Chequers nightclub in Sydney in 1963, shows Dad with the ballerina celebrating with Aubrey, Uncle Les and his wife, Thelma. Aubrey was very unhappy with this match, too. Of course, she was Caucasian.

Dad started work as soon as the family moved back to Sydney from Minnesota in 1972. A salary slip from that time states that he was paid $44 per week for his job as staff specialist cardiothoracic surgeon. Mum says the family was really struggling. We stayed in several places before eventually settling in Clontarf. Our first accommodation in Sydney was an apartment in Manly. Mum didn't know where Manly was, but she organised for the family to move there anyway. When the bedbugs got to her, we moved again. They signed a six-month lease on a house in Clontarf. Coincidentally, that house is directly opposite our current family house and the gentleman who leased the house to Mum and Dad was Derryn Hinch.

Dad's constant moving and travelling didn't seem to drain him of energy. He had very early starts each morning and was always on call. With his childhood experiences of moving from city to city during World War Two, he was probably accustomed to it. Those experiences also taught him the importance of not going hungry. It was rare for a day to pass by without him eating rice. Upon observing this one day, Dad's friend Dr Saw asked him about it. Dad's reply was: 'Rice tells you that there is peace—if you can get rice when you want rice, there is peace. If you can't get rice when you want rice, then you are in the midst of unrest.' He used to tell me that for every grain in my bowl, there would be a starving child in the world. Even now I make sure I devour every grain in my bowl and I feel guilty if any goes to waste.

Possibly his need to feel secure contributed to his love of collecting beautiful objects. His passion for cars extended to his set of miniature cars, all faithful replicas of original models. He knew that every birthday he would receive a new one from one of his children. He also loved antiques. When I was twelve years old, Mum and Dad introduced me to Asian artefacts. We were in Singapore at the time, spending days raking through antique shops in search of the perfect Tang horse or a flawless Ming vase. Dad had a real appreciation for unusual pieces; he and Mum often studied Chinese antiques upstairs in the study, pouring through a multitude of books and speaking with excited voices about their latest acquisition.

There were other splendours from Asia: rugs and carpets from Persia and Afghanistan, some tribal, others in silk, wool, cashmere or cotton. We spent many nights luxuriating on sample rugs brought to the house for the family to assess, lie on, study, turn over, run our fingers through and tread upon. It was all fun; Dad loved it.

My father didn't have much time in his life for leisure activities. Exercise wasn't his thing, although when he had lived with his cousins in Campsie, he had played competition tennis every weekend. Apparently he was a very good player. I seem to recall a large collection of Kennex racquets gathering dust up in his cupboard. He had intended to play when he got older, but there was just never enough time.

His ambition for me was that I would become a champion swimmer, so he baptised me in a very cold pool at a very young age. I sank and cried. Then when my brothers and I grew more accustomed to the water, Dad would take us to the Forum swimming pool in Collaroy to do laps. His work seemed to keep him fit and miraculously he didn't seem to age. He didn't have one grey hair on his head and he had very few wrinkles. He was youthful and energetic, which made him seem many years younger than he actually was.

Very conscious of the ageing process, I think he was dreading the effects of age on his body. His father Aubrey used to drink snake oil to preserve himself, but I don't think Dad went to the same lengths. When he spoke of growing old, he would tell me that he'd want to die peacefully in his sleep. He related one story to me over and over, the story of one of his patients. The old gentleman was dying and he had a very loving daughter, who kept a bedside vigil. She held his hand day after day, waiting for him to go. Dad wanted the same devotion from me.

He may have had insecurities about his role in the family. If he did, it was because he was conscious of the time he spent away from us. But he had the love of his children. We accompanied him through hospital corridors from a very young age, doing the rounds with him at Cameron Wing, visiting his patients, learning how to take blood pressure and use the stethoscope. I am transported back to my childhood whenever I step into a hospital, overcome by nostalgia when I encounter that familiar clinical smell. It reminds me of my father.

In hospital, there were sad times, too. Not all

patients lived after an operation and then there was always the possibility of post-operative complications. Dad had failures; he lost patients, and he was sad about each one. It didn't happen very often, but when it did he would walk in the front door and be visibly upset. I can't remember ever actually seeing him cry, but losing a patient was probably as close to crying as he ever got.

In April 1991 I was in Germany. I had been travelling around Europe for a year and I had a job in Dusseldorf, teaching two children English. Dad called and said he wanted to treat me to a little holiday—he asked whether I would meet him and Mum in London. We'd go to Cambridge, spend some time in London, then fly to Geneva to see the famous annual motor show there. We did all that. On the morning before my parents were due to leave, my father practically begged me to fly back to Sydney with them. He promised he'd give me a return ticket to Germany, so long as I came back just for a little while to spend time with the family. I don't know why I agreed to it, but suddenly I was packing my bags to join them on the flight that afternoon. It was impulsive; I had to call my employer to let him know I'd be back soon and I left luggage in England, which I only retrieved on a visit ten years later.

Dad was overjoyed that I agreed to go home with him and Mum. He hugged me for it, and said the words, 'I love you, daughter.' I returned his affection.

It was an unusual exchange, which is why I remember it so clearly. I never returned to Europe, and three months later he was gone forever. It was the best decision I ever made.

8

Teacher and team

Dad strongly believed that to be truly successful in life, people should pass on their knowledge and expertise. For your work to develop and be remembered, the most important thing was to teach, to pass on your skills to others so they could continue without you. He felt there was nothing to be gained by keeping knowledge to yourself.

Over the years, he trained cardiac surgical registrars from within Australia and also from overseas. Guan Chong, his colleague from the Mayo Clinic, says this was one of the most valuable things he learnt from my father. Harry Windsor, Dad's mentor, also endorsed this philosophy. Harry had even placed a quote—from renowned surgeon Lord Moynihan—in the foyer of Cameron Wing, stating that the best surgeon was one who taught others to be better than himself.

The teaching aspect of my father's job was a deeply satisfying part of his life. He loved having protégés, not because he 'made' them, but because they could then train others in the same way he had. Of course, there would have been a certain amount of self-pride attached to seeing these young, unsure trainees develop into talented, confident surgeons, but I don't think it was self-centred pride.

The job of training overseas visitors went much further than simply coaching the budding surgeon or nurse. He embraced the challenge in a holistic way, so that all the aspects of moving them to Australia were satisfied. Having been a migrant himself, Dad understood the stress people experienced when they left their homeland and relocated, often without their families, to learn the finer techniques of surgery. He strived to create an environment that was as comfortable as possible for them.

These visiting doctors and nurses would often come to our home to share a meal with us, or join us over the weekend. I arrived home many times to a house full of foreign faces—Chinese, Indian, Japanese and Singaporean. Our home was, and still is, open to many 'homeless' visitors to this country.

I was always interested to hear of the experiences of one of Dad's trainees, through his or her eyes. Ulla, a nurse who trained under Dad, worked with him for years afterwards. Of these times, she said,

> We were a very happy family. First, Victor would make sure that each of the visiting trainee doctors and support staff would have somewhere pleasant to

live. We all helped to create a homely and welcoming atmosphere so that the doctors, nurses and other staff felt as much at home as possible. He frequently threw parties for all of us. He understood the difficulties experienced by overseas doctors and nurses and although he gave the impression of a man dedicated only to his profession . . . he cared deeply about the emotional and physical well-being of his colleagues and their families.

There were so many trainee doctors that I couldn't possibly have asked all of them to tell their story. I contacted Dr B.V. Rama Rao, now Surgeon-in-Chief and Chairman and founder of the Victor Chang Heart Institute and Research Centre in Hyderabad, India. My father once said that this man was one of the most talented surgeons to have ever trained under him.

Rao was sent to train under Dad in 1984 after completing his training in India. He came to Sydney to 'learn the finer points of cardiac surgery under the Master from the East'. I asked him about how he came to meet my father and what he learnt. He had this to say:

The very first day at St Vincent's was a revelation about the way the Master worked. As I arrived at the old Cameron Wing lifts, there was the Master, also waiting at the lift on his way to . . . an emergency in the Operating Room [OR]. He enquired who I was and when I proudly told him, 'I have come here to train under Dr Chang,' he flashed his brilliant smile, shook hands with me and said, 'Hey Rao, I am Victor, come with me to the OR, there is an emergency.' After fourteen hours and three continuous operations with no break, this shell-shocked youngster realised the pace which the Master sets for his disciples is like a rigorous workout for an aspiring Olympian. Thus started my relationship with the teacher that not only fulfilled [my] wish . . . to achieve skills in cardiothoracic surgery but also helped [me] attain a philosophy of life. I say this because there are many good teachers who could train you to operate, but this Master taught his wards the finer points of cardiac surgery [and] also how to do the walk of life with confidence and verve.

Rao quoted two examples of Dad's advice. The first concerns focus. One day Dad told him that if you set yourself a goal it can be achieved by untiring persever-ance. He gave an example of a drop of rain, saying, 'Rao, a drop of rain has only one destination: the sea. On its journey it joins like-minded drops, forming a stream, then a rivulet, a tributary and finally it becomes a river as it relentlessly marches towards the sea. On its journey it encounters many obstacles such as mountains but it still continues to march towards the sea.' From such examples, Dad taught Rao about focus and perseverance.

The second piece of advice was about achieving the unachievable. Dad was operating on a very sick person who was turned down by all the big names in the US. Rao asked him, 'Sir, don't you think you are taking a high-risk case?' Dad replied, 'Rao, the risk is all in the surgeon's mind. A difficult mathematical equation might have only one way to arrive at an answer, unlike an easy sum which may have multiple ways of arriving at the answer. Only by careful and organised thought processes can you arrive at the correct answer.' Rao continues:

[Mr Chang] said that the immense potential of the mind can make things happen if you think, and also that every time you achieve something, you have to raise an extra inch on the crossbar to achieve higher goals . . . .Was he just a relentless driver of people to achieve only professional goals? Certainly not. I realised that Mr Chang intentionally instilled . . . extra elements in his teachings to prepare us for a higher cause . . . His concern for these youngsters who came to St Vincent's from all over the world went beyond the training. Behind the uncompromising and firm will to make his wards equal to the best in the world there was a genuine and humane concern for their welfare. All the team at St Vincent's created an atmosphere conducive to the all-round development of young surgeons, especially the trainees from overseas . . .

Everyone made such an effort to help these overseas trainees overcome any shortcomings during their training, plus on the weekends took them to their family lunches . . . giving them lots of social and moral support. Mr Chang would always help these youngsters to gain the best from each of the teachers and I am sure that he exchanged notes with all his teammates on how best to help these trainees with diverse backgrounds. Mr Chang proved, beyond doubt, that hidden potential in people could be brought out by gentle manoeuvring of the person to overcome fears and inhibitions and by creating conditions which helped him realise his/her full potential.

Rao says that apart from the training at the workplace, the trainees were also given financial and other social support, especially the Chinese and Indian trainees who were from different ethnic and cultural back-grounds. He says the care he and the trainees were shown by everyone at St Vincent's left a very deep impression in their hearts.

It created an enormous amount of goodwill for Australia and Australians in the countries from where these trainees came. [Mr Chang's] concern for the welfare of their families extended far beyond the call of duty as a teacher. St Vincent's . . . always felt [like] a home away from home.

Mr Chang also showed us how the right team spirit could be built in spite of the high-voltage personalities in the cardiac team. He had genuine praise and admiration for his colleagues. He would say, 'Rao, don't you think Alan [Dr Farnsworth] is Mach 3 when all of us are only Mach 1?' This kind of open admiration for a colleague in sadly lacking in many teams all over the world.

He would strive to make extra effort to reach out to individuals, without expecting any returns. Once when I thanked him for providing me the opportunity to come to train at St Vincent's, he told me, 'Rao, somebody helped me and I try to help you, and you've got to help someone else so that we could make the world a better place to live in.' In January 1989, when I was leaving the shores of Australia along with my wife and my first son, Sita Ram Victor, Mr Chang insisted on dropping me and my family at the airport in his car. This testifies to the humility of this great soul, who gave his time and energies so generously. As I was departing he shook my hand and in a very emotional tone told me, 'Rao take good care of the little boy.' When I was back in India, he would frequently call and enquire how I was settling in my new job.

After Mr Chang's death, I set up the Victor Chang Heart Institute and Research Centre at Hyderabad, India, which is mainly sponsored by my patients. In the short span of a few years, A\$200,000 worth of free treatment was rendered to underprivileged patients. We have also embarked on continued medical education and instituted the Victor Chang Travelling Fellowship for training young surgeons, cardiologists and perfusionists. Mr Mark Shanahan delivered the very first Victor Chang Memorial Lecture four years ago. A preventive cardiac care program has also been launched in the form of the Victor Chang Preventive Cardiac Care Program, which helps identify high-risk individuals for heart disease and provides information regarding risk factor management . . . to control or decrease the incidence of fatal heart attacks. I am sure the late Mr Chang would approve of all this.

As with most professionals, Dad never stopped educating himself and he wanted the same for his staff, trainees, family and patients. He once said in an interview,

It is not necessary to think that by going overseas you will become a better technical surgeon, in fact, you probably won't, but what you will learn will be discipline and intellectual stimulation. It has always been my philosophy to get re-educated at least once a year by attending one, maybe two, major international meetings in cardiothoracic surgery.

He did attend many overseas meetings and while he was gone, the team at St Vincent's worked hard. I often wonder how they felt about Dad as a 'boss' and about the attention he received in the media—attention that was unwanted most of the time. Did they feel as though he was the only person getting all the accolades? So many of the people I have spoken with have referred to the team as a family. So I would hope, as would Dad, that other team members did not feel disgruntled about his name being shouted from the headlines. He did much in his life to avoid this from happening.

Michael McBride, from the heart-transplant team in the earlier years, said that Dad was very much a team person and always shared any accolades that came his way with staff in the Heart–Lung Transplant Unit, and all St Vincent's staff. Without the support from the various sections of the hospital, the work of the HLTU would not have become the success it did. Staff on the very busy St Vincent's switchboard often told me how wonderful he was—never rude and always showed his appreciation of their efforts.

When he received an award, he would insist that it was team effort that helped him to achieve that award and therefore it belonged to the team. He explained his approach to team-building in an interview, when he said that cardiac surgery is entirely teamwork; no one person should take credit for everything.

The support staff is integral to the whole cardiac surgery unit . . . the physicians who assess your patients before the operation, the anaesthetic department, the perfusion department, the nursing care after surgery and pre-operatively are all important and must be first-rate in order to get consistently good results. The job of the surgeon, apart from doing a good operation, is to motivate your team in such a way that he can bring out the best from the people who work with you.

In practice, Michael McBride said she felt that Dad always gave his best and he expected the same from those working with him. If the job was not carried out properly, he would let everyone know in no uncertain terms and all would experience his wrath. This was not something that Michael ever experienced herself, but she knows of colleagues who did, explaining that his anger would be over quickly, but everyone tried very hard not to offend again!

In the same way that my family functioned—never experiencing a dull moment living with Dad—so the team at the hospital functioned. Michael tells me that it was a very rewarding experience and one she will never forget.

It's difficult to adequately describe the complexities that made Victor the person he was, with the charisma that attracted people to him. There were times of fun—he had a good sense of humour—sadness, anger, frustration and excellence, amongst a lot of hard work on 24-hour call, seven days a week. Although he was 'the boss', he was also a friend. If teased about something he would briefly get a small quizzical frown between the eyebrows while assessing if you were joking or serious!

Yet, both in his life and in his death, Victor made the greatest change of all, to everyone whose life he had touched . . . [he would have had the same effect on] those who would have come to him in the future, to learn, or to be healed by his skills.

The one thing Dad said he hated most was change. He really disliked it when someone working with him moved away. Michael was one of those who did just that, in 1990. He told her, 'It's not the same!' He liked the camaraderie and the security of working with people he knew and trusted.

9

Ambassador

On a clear, sunny day in March 1986, the Queen of England presented a group of proud Australians with an Order of Australia. Some received awards for bravery, some for literature or service to the community. Dad was awarded a Companion to the Order of Australia (AC) for 'service to international relations between Australia and China and to medical science'. I travelled with Mum and Dad to Canberra to watch Dad accept the award; it was one of many he would be presented with in his lifetime, but this one was different because it acknowledged his contribution to Australia–China relations and his unofficial role as Australia's medical ambassador to Asia.

The work Dad performed in Australia on heart-transplant patients changed his life forever; from the early '80s he was unable to escape media attention. Journalists typically described him as a shy, self-effacing man. As I've mentioned, he refused to answer any questions of a personal nature and he often asked the media to acknowledge the team, not the individual.

His work in Asia was not as well publicised in Australia, but it was something he found deeply fulfilling. He felt strong ties with the country of his birth and despite living in Australia for most of his life, he was always a Chinaman, and he held the values of the Chinese.

When Dad's family fled Shanghai in 1937, he was an eight-month-old baby. He returned four decades later for the first time as an adult, as a 40-year-old visiting doctor. It was a turning point in his career. After visiting a Chinese ambassador with heart trouble in hospital, the Chinese Government invited him to visit his birthplace as a gesture of thanks. Dad, being deeply conscious of his Chinese heritage, was very happy to accept the invitation and the trip took place in 1977.

He said in an interview in 1983, 'I am basically Chinese and I feel I have an obligation to make a contribution to my own people. When the mainland Chinese Government first approached me, they knew all about me and my family. I was very pleased. It didn't worry them that I am a capitalist. With me, politics comes last.'

Unofficially, it was a chance for Dad to assess China's standard of cardiac surgery and equipment. He was horrified by what he saw. In illustrating the antiquated condition of their hospitals, he related the story of a little girl he found lying in the corridors. He was being escorted through the hospital to inspect all the facilities. He noticed a young girl, a patient of about seven or eight, lying motionless with a dark grey complexion. He stopped to feel her pulse, but those who were escorting him hurried him on; they thought she was unimportant and beyond help. Dad continued to inspect the operating theatres and on his way back, stopped to see the little girl again. He examined her and suspected she had a hole in her heart. He asked if the theatre could be opened so he could operate immediately. His diagnosis was correct and he repaired the hole that day. Upon his return, two days later, the little girl was pink-cheeked and chatting with her parents, who, upon seeing Dad, bowed down to him, thanking him for saving their child. When he visited the next year, the whole family turned up at the airport to greet him!

My father estimated that the Chinese hospitals were about fifteen years behind the rest of the world with their cardiac technology. On the same visit that saw him operate on the little girl, he was asked to attend an operation during which the patient was not anaesthetised in the way Westerners know it. The hospital staff were feeding the patient—who was conscious—with mandarin segments. At the same time, the treatment included acupuncture. Dad watched in amazement as surgery took place using these methods. After the operation, the patient was able to get out of bed and walk.

This shocked him, and he told them so. As a result, he was officially asked to help upgrade the standards of cardiac surgery in China. He agreed to help. And so began a cultural and intellectual exchange program between China and Australia which helped in a small way to cement better relations between the two countries. It involved the training of Chinese surgeons in Australia under the tutelage of Dad and the whole St Vincent's team. They would take home what they learnt and pass this knowledge on to other surgeons in China.

In 1978, the first Chinese surgeon was invited to Australia, and thereafter, between one and two surgeons from the more needy institutions in China visited Australia each year to work and learn with Dad's team. This took place shortly after the opening of China to the West; Australian Foreign Affairs officers had been making slow progress towards improving relations with China, so the St Vincent's Hospital initiative augured well for Australia–China relations. This was recognised in 1986 when Dad received his AC.

After his visit in 1977, Dad started making annual trips to China. Taking his own delegation of surgeons, nurses and other specialists, he would stay for at least two weeks at a time. He would operate and lecture in Beijing and around China, and would delight in sightseeing and playing guide to the team. On one of these trips, Dad invited John Gosage, the official hospital photographer, telling him he was the first medical photographer from the West to visit China. John captured Dad's happiness in being 'home' and documented the trip beautifully in colour, as well as black and white.

My father asked me many times to accompany him on one of these trips, but I was always too busy. I intended to wait until I was older, so I deeply regret not being able to see China with him, stand on the Great Wall and visit his birthplace.

Professor Don Harrison, at the time an anaesthetist at St Vincent's Hospital, shared many of these excursions with the team, not only to China, but to Hong Kong, Singapore and Indonesia. Professor Harrison called them 'adventures' because of the challenges they faced in the introduction or refinement of techniques of cardiac surgery that were much less optimal than they were accustomed to. Pressures to succeed were great and sometimes onerous. On one level, teams were honoured guests sharing their professional skills but on another level, best known to my father, there were pressures—political, professional, academic, social, sometimes even international—that added an edge to many of the trips. Professor Harrison continues:

These journeys brought out a side of Victor's personality that most of his professional colleagues experienced little of in our usual environment. It was the human side that I remember most. Victor was a resourceful leader but even more, a delightful travelling companion. He was [intensely] proud of his Chinese roots. He studied Chinese history— social, political, artistic and medical—and shared his insights freely with us on the long plane trips. The photographs show a happy man. Victor [was] relaxed and completely at ease, showing off his spiritual home to his colleagues: the Great Wall; in the Summer Palace; at a gathering to honour his surgical contributions; and outside the Fu Wai Hospital with its admiring staff. He was equally relaxed and at home in the sophisticated environs of Singapore and Hong Kong where his reputation as a quality surgeon was very high.

Earlier I mentioned that Dad's birth was recorded in a special book. Dad related the wonderful story that follows to Sixth Aunt when he returned from one of his visits to China.

It must have been on one of his initial trips to Shanghai, and Dad was keen to trace the exact place and time of his birth. The hospital he was born in was notified and a visit from Dad and his entourage was organised, with maximum pomp. The hospital staff were excited because they had managed to locate the central birth register of the year: 1936. On the day, Dad and his team arrived in a minibus and the official welcome concluded with a flourish as they opened the book to the relevant date and presented it to him. Horrors! His name did not appear among the births. The mood in the minibus on the way home was very subdued and everyone was perplexed by what had happened. Dad sloped into the hotel with his head down, unable to hide his great disappointment. Some time later he was contacted again and told that his name *had* been discovered, but not in the General

Birth Book. 'Chang, Yam Him' had been recorded in the Instrumental Delivery Book, which was reserved for 'special births' requiring forceps. Dad was relieved, delighted and extremely proud of that one small entry in a very long list of names. He often spoke of the significance of the event for him, despite the fact that he never actually saw it. This small incident ranked among the most valued experiences of his lifetime.

In Sydney in the early 1980s, Dad arranged to meet a delegation of Chinese cardiac specialists, led by Tao Shu Chi, the pioneer of modern cardiology in China. Tao had studied at Harvard with Paul Dudley White, who was physician to Dwight Eisenhower after the latter suffered a heart attack. Tao, who had attended Chinese leader Zhou En Lai and Mao Zhedong, was a quiet, charming man. I have heard many people describe my father using the same words and, like Dad, Tao was very open about China and its problems. Tao's visit to St Vincent's was followed by a succession of visits by Chinese cardiac surgeons and cardiologists.

When Dad and his team—including a cardiologist, intensivist, nurse educator and intensive care nurse—travelled to Chinese cardiac centres, he insisted that they all split up and work independently with their Chinese colleagues. One of Dad's colleagues, cardiologist Michael O'Rourke, was impressed by the enthusiasm of his Chinese colleagues, their humility, their desire to learn and their work with the primitive equipment they had. He told me how he felt on his first trip.

> Victor was a great leader. His work was superb, and he got the best from us all. We also had great fun. Out of hours he told stories, each more far-fetched than the last. We were prompted to reciprocate . . . we laughed and laughed. Our hosts insisted that we sightsee, in the company of those with whom we worked. This trip to China was one of the greatest experiences of my life. My lasting memory was of friendly, enthusiastic people emerging from an awkward past, with noble traditions and a great optimism for the future. Again, without Victor, my life would have been poorer. Victor's trips to China continued but, as in Singapore, their facilities and training continued to improve, and the need for our presence lessened.

In 1983, Dad's contribution to the development of medicine in China was recognised by the Chinese Government when he was officially thanked by Premier Zhao Ziyang in Beijing. He was also made honorary professor at various Chinese institutions. What pleased him most was the fact that the recognition had come from the land of his ancestors, mainland China, his spiritual home.

All around Asia, Dad was invited to advise on and open clinics. He had become a pre-eminent heart surgeon in the region and operated on many high-profile patients. I won't name them here because if Dad were alive he wouldn't want me to draw attention to this!

In 1984, Indonesian President Suharto and his wife commissioned the building of a modern hospital in Jakarta. A centrepiece of the hospital was to be a national cardiac centre. Arrangements were made with the renowned Dr De Bakey from Baylor College in Houston and his team to establish the centre, and it was to be called Rumah Sakit Jantung Harapan Kita (Our Hope Heart Hospital). Soon after it opened, though, eight tragic deaths occurred after surgery. Patients fled the hospital and morale collapsed among both staff and surgeons. The hospital was closed and the surgical team was sent back to the US.

Investigations revealed that contaminated fluids had caused the patients' deaths. Almost a year later, Dad was asked to advise and help rehabilitate the centre for re-opening. Problems were identified and corrected, staff were retrained and he came back with a team of nurses and doctors to recommence the surgical program. The centre was re-opened and Dad was involved in the first thirteen operations. He returned to Harapan Kita every three months for eighteen months. It is now the leading heart centre in Indonesia, performing 1200 cardiac operations every year.

Dad's opinion of his own contribution was not quite so high. In 1987 he wrote a paper addressed to the Ministry of Health in Singapore, entitled 'Progress of Cardiac Surgery in Singapore'. In it he reported, 'Harapan Kita was completed in 1985 and although they had a difficult start in May 1986, the cardiac surgery is now running relatively smoothly. I have played a small role in helping to re-establish the reputation of the centre in adult cardiac surgery . . .'

Years later, a party was given in Dad's honour at the Indonesian Presidential Palace by the Minister for Health. Dad was thanked formally for 'rehabilitating' the Harapan Kita. The minister added very deliberately that Dad had also 'rehabilitated' Australia's relationship with Indonesia on account of the many other ways, direct and indirect, that he had helped smooth difficulties and provided liaison at many levels of society. This position was closely observed by the Australian Government, and was one of the reasons for his award as Australian of the Year in 1985. Dad's colleagues tell me that all of this was done with Dad playing down his own efforts. Laughing, he would say things like, 'Who is this fellow they are talking about?'

The photos taken at the Presidential Palace show Dad and his colleagues in batik shirts singing along with the whole gathering. Characteristically, Dad behaved with formality during official speeches and toasts, and in the operating room at critical periods, but it was always mixed with laughter, practical jokes and merriment. He remained the official advisor on cardiac training to the Indonesian Government until his death.

I have a letter from Australia's then prime minister, Bob Hawke, written on 10 February 1987. It reads:

It has come to my notice that you were involved in heart surgery at the Harapan Kita Cardiac Centre in Jakarta and that the Indonesians are very impressed by and appreciative of your invaluable work. I would like to take this opportunity to congratulate you on the thirteen heart bypass operations that you successfully conducted at the Centre.

H. Alamsjah Ratu Perwiranegara, Indonesia's Minister Coordinator for People's Welfare, whom you operated on in Singapore last August, wrote to me expressing his appreciation to you and your team for your excellent work and care while he was in hospital. I understand that he has recently shown his personal gratitude by honouring you with the Lampung title 'Pengirn Ratu'.

It is a pleasure to see an individual, by contributing his expertise, simultaneously helping to save human lives and at the same time bringing honour to himself and to his country. I believe individuals can and do play an important part in fostering understanding between nations. Australia can only benefit from the goodwill which results from your invaluable work at the Centre and I would like to express my personal thanks for this.

Despite the many positive stories involving my father and his work, especially in Asia, there were also negative elements at play. My father was most aware of ill-feeling from some of his peers and competitors. He liked to be liked and often lamented any rivalry he may have inadvertently caused. He certainly felt the presence of this negative force, in both Singapore and Indonesia. Dad's close colleague and confidant from Singapore, Dr Saw Huat Seong, says that there was a group of 'watchers' who were either envious or jealous. Dad was watched by these people and bad-mouthed every step of the way. 'They begrudged him the fame and accolades he received . . . Not once was Victor complimented [by his Indonesian peers] on what he brought to Jakarta . . .'

Professional jealousies will always exist, my father knew that, but he saw no point in confronting them or letting them hinder his work in Asia. Aware of the issues, however, he wrote in the conclusion of his paper, 'Progress of Cardiac Surgery in Singapore', 'I would be pleased to continue my role as advisor in the form of regular visits if this is the wish of your government, but I would be equally pleased if you would kindly inform me once this role is to be relinquished.' He was never asked to do so.

For many years, Singapore was like a home to me. I first travelled there with Mum and Dad in 1981. In 1986, my final year in school, our family would have many conversations about a possible permanent relocation there. We decided against it because it was too disruptive for our education, particularly since I was in my final year of high school.

Dad helped initiate, consolidate and promote the

Singapore General Hospital's coronary artery bypass surgical program. He operated and taught often during 1982 and 1983. Rather than have the more affluent patients travel to him in Sydney, he encouraged them to undergo surgery led by him alongside local surgeons in the private sector, first at the Mount Elizabeth Hospital and later at the Gleneagles Hospital. This way, local patients felt more comfortable about having their surgery performed 'at home'. Post-operative treatment went hand in hand with the involvement of staff from St Vincent's Hospital alongside local staff.

After he oversaw the various phases of its development, Singapore's National University Hospital (NUH) performed its first open-heart surgery under Dad's supervision in December 1986. In January 1987, he took his team to NUH to consolidate the program, and for that he was made a visiting professor. As in Indonesia, he made arrangements for Singaporean nurses and doctors to have extended training periods at St Vincent's.

After observing the success of Singapore's private-practice cardiac surgical program, staff at the Pranti Medical Centre in Malaysia contacted Dad in 1988, inviting him to launch their open-heart surgery program. Dad led a team from St Vincent's, comprising Dr Phil Spratt, current Director of the Heart–Lung Transplant Unit in Sydney, Professor Don Harrison, Dr Frank Junius and two nurses, to Kuala Lumpur. Dad left soon after the program was launched; the team then took over with Dr Spratt in charge.

Dad always felt that Hong Kong had the potential to open a good cardiac unit, commenting, 'If Thailand can do it and Taiwan can do it, so can Hong Kong.' However, no request came from Hong Kong in his lifetime and so his trips were primarily to visit his father. He did a little work there, operating on a few patients and training up three surgeons.

In one of the very few television interviews Dad agreed to give, he expressed his opinions on Australia's relationship with Asia and why he thought Asian people gravitated to him. He said:

> [Asians] think Australia wants to be an outpost of
> Europe. I try to tell them no, our politicians and our
> prime minister [have] always said that we are part of
> Asia and we want to play a major role in Asia and we
> can, in terms of medical and technical, and in other
> areas too . . . A person of their own race may have a
> better understanding of their customs, their culture
> and their requirements and they are probably more
> tolerant of their shortcomings, and I am, compared
> with some of the people that they . . . get from the US.

One of the last international activities Dad took on was to advise the Japanese Government on heart transplantation. Japanese culture did not readily accept organ donation and Dad, a person with similar values who had successfully initiated a heart transplant program, was of particular assistance to the Japanese.

Training of overseas doctors, from China and other Asian nations, continues at St Vincent's Hospital in Sydney.

10

Inventor

Dad liked to know how things worked, what made them tick, and he liked solving problems, the harder and more challenging, the better. As a young boy he created models from scratch, not relying on a set of instructions to help him. He had a blueprint in his mind which he used to construct his vision. The need to use his hands was sated through surgery and he used his mind to invent. The artificial heart and the St Vincent's valve are two examples of this. He also used his knowledge and experience to try constantly to improve upon his own surgical techniques. Sometimes his patients were the catalyst for new ideas, such as the 'bikini cut girl', Julie Meldrum.

Julie told me her story recently, and since then I have read two articles that mention the bikini cut technique. In February 1977, at the age of twenty, Julie was diagnosed with an atrial septal defect (ASD), or hole in the heart, that had remained undetected until then. She was living in Canberra and was in the final year of a three-year journalism cadetship at the *Canberra Times*. There weren't the facilities or expertise in Canberra to rectify the problem, so she was referred to St Vincent's. Dad was assigned as her surgeon, along with Dr Harry Windsor. The ASD was larger than they had originally thought. Her health was deteriorating rapidly, so they booked her in for the operation in early March.

In hospital, Julie found that she was surrounded by much older people who had already undergone heart surgery. She called them the 'zipper people', because they were all marked with a prominent horizontal chest scar. In Indonesia many years later, one of Dad's patients would start up the Zebra Club, named for their striped scars. Dad was the patron!

An independent young girl, Julie decided she didn't want one of those scars, which she regarded as a huge disfigurement. Also, as she already knew that her skin had a tendency to scar as a keloid (raised scar), so she was doubly concerned. She relayed her fears to Dad, who understood her apprehension. When he visited her the next day, one day before the operation, he wasn't his normal, high-energy self. He'd been up all night thinking about her request and he'd come up with a solution to the problem. He would make the incision under the right breast, then he would access the heart through a cut sternum. This would leave a subtle scar that folded into the natural lines of a woman's body, directly under the breast. Surgery went ahead, and though the operation was longer than usual because of the pioneering nature of the cut, it was successful. From that day on she was known to Dad as the 'bikini cut girl'. He went on to use this technique for other patients undergoing this type of surgery. On 19 July 1991, two weeks after Dad's death, Julie went into labour in Hong Kong, where she was living at the time. Outside, on Hong Kong Harbour, Typhoon Victor had arrived.

During one of Dad's early trips to China in the late 1970s, he realised the number of people there suffering from heart disease, especially valvular and congenital heart disease, was enormous. These people were dying because they couldn't afford the operation to receive expensive American- and European-made heart valves (presently costing over A$3000). Being a mechanically minded person who enjoyed the process of trial, experimentation and invention, Dad had already started to think about the possibility of a new heart valve, one that would not be as expensive as the imported models. At first, Dad was interested in the use of a non-mechanical valve, a 'bovine pericardial valve', to be tested on selected patients in Australia. This valve would prove to be very effective.

A bovine pericardial valve is made from beef pericardium (the sac around the heart that keeps it in place), and it is easy to obtain. It is coated with gluteraldehyde, also used for tanning leather, which binds the proteins so that they don't act as antibodies and react against the body. These valves are inexpensive in comparison with prosthetic valves, which are made from metals, plastic or carbon—all expensive materials that take longer to rework.

In 1980 he met Frank Tamru, a heart valve specialist working in the Asia-Pacific region for a company called Shiley Inc. Frank remembers the day Dad said to him, 'Why don't we make our own valves for Asian patients? We can do this cheaper and just as well as the established companies.' Frank wasn't surprised by the confidence Dad showed in making these statements. He continues:

> I had been transferred to Hong Kong to help open the China market for the valves and this motivated Victor even more to pursue his dream of providing low-cost valves for Asian patients, made in Asia . . . by Asian workers. He knew we could convince an Indian tissue valve engineer [Brij Gupta] . . . at Shiley to join our project, especially after I mentioned [Victor's] desire to provide a good, affordable tissue valve for . . . [people in his] homeland.

Brij Gupta and Dad met at an American cardiac meeting in early 1983 and the first words from my father's mouth were: 'Please join us in this project, let's work together to make our dreams come true.' Without hesitation the young Indian became part of the emerging 'group'.

In 1985 Dad wrote a three-page letter to Neville Wran about the various projects he was undertaking with St Vincent's. One involved the manufacture of valves, to be marketed in China and exported to South-East Asia. In his correspondence to Wran he added that he didn't want any personal credit for the development of the two valves. He requested they be named the St Vincent's Tissue Valve and the St Vincent's Mechanical Valve.

Back at St Vincent's, working in converted nurses' quarters, Dad set up a makeshift laboratory, and began to assemble a group of international specialists in various fields. The research team was based in the lab to test materials for the manufacture of the St Vincent's Mechanical Valve, and, more importantly, to push ahead with the development of Dad's long-held dream, the creation of a low-cost artificial heart.

The artificial heart would be an Australian invention, but it would also suit patients in China and the developing world who couldn't afford Western donor heart-transplant technology. By having either two or four inexpensive valves in either a Left Ventricular Assist Device (LVAD) or Total Artificial Heart (TAH), the production cost would drop significantly. This idea enthralled Dad and motivated him to move forward immediately. The LVAD is a way of supporting patients whose hearts aren't strong enough to pump blood fully on their own—it relieves some of the workload. The TAH is intended for patients with imminent heart failure who are awaiting heart transplantation. It also has a temporary function for those with hearts that need time to recover their pumping power. The TAH can either be implanted in a patient's body, or used externally.

Essentially, an artificial heart is a blood pump. Dad saw it as a standard piece of surgical equipment that should, one day, be available in all cardiac units. It could also be used for transplant patients while they waited for a suitable donor heart.

Dad soon started adding to the small team he'd gathered, enlisting the help of Professor Ye Chun-Xiu, a doctor visiting from China. Professor Ye had already worked on an innovative 'spiral vortex' design for a blood pump which he hadn't brought to fruition. The spiral vortex works on the same principle as water in a sink flowing down the plughole: it swirls around before it enters the hole; with blood, it is important that the swirl is continuous or clotting occurs. Dad was then introduced to a talented young Japanese engineer, Dr Mitsuo Umezu, a specialist in heart valve development and blood flow dynamics—both essential for producing a successful replacement heart or blood pump. It was 1987 and Dr Umezu was already at work designing a heart pump in Japan.

Dad described his dream of building an Australian artificial heart to the young engineer. The first question Dr Umezu asked was, 'What is a major reason to select me? There are many competitive, brilliant artificial heart researchers in the USA.' Dad's response was that Dr Umezu had unique experience in artificial heart research from a biomedical engineering point of view, and he wanted to learn this knowledge from him. Then, Dr Umezu said, 'It is hard for me to communicate in English. What do you think of this matter?' Dad replied that he wanted Dr Umezu for his experience, not for his English. Dr Umezu said Dad's 'balanced "way of thinking" between Western and oriental' always impressed him.

The last additions to the team were an administrative coordinator, Kay Pittlekow, a Canadian biomedical engineer, Allen Nugent, and a clinical nurse coordinator, Sister Fiona Aitchison.

In 1990, after three years of research on variables such as material, internal shapes, positioning of outflow and inflow tubes, flow of fluid through the chambers and texture quality of the internal surface, the team's artificial heart—the fifth prototype they created—was ready for clinical testing. Real blood needed to be pushed through the heart, which is cone-shaped with two tubes extending from it, and live animals also needed to be used for trial runs.

The artificial heart, in reality, would be grafted onto arteries and veins from the natural heart and would be connected to a large metal box, an external power console, that forced air into the heart and then sucked it out again. The total cost of the heart was about A$5000, plus about another A$25,000 for the large metal console. The testing was done on a sheep and one of Dad's ex-patients, Tom Hayson, was there to witness it.

One day [Victor] rang and said, 'I want you to come with me while I try out my new Mercedes, and I will show you something special.' Driving with Victor in his new cars was always a thrill, but I will never forget where we went on that day and what I saw.

Our destination was the old Prince Henry Hospital at Long Bay near La Perouse. In a ward that had been turned over to his exclusive use, history was being enacted. The characters—Victor, [along with] a Chinese heart specialist assistant he had brought over from China and 'Daisy' (I think [the sheep] was called 'Daisy') . . . which had been surviving for over two weeks with an artificial heart!

Dad was hopeful that within eighteen months the heart would be ready for use on humans. He was about to start looking for more funds to continue research, testing and production but, sadly, when his life ended, so did his work on the artificial heart. Technology has probably now superseded the old design but I hope one day, somewhere in Australia—he wanted it to be an Australian invention—someone will be interested enough to take up this project again and raise the funds necessary to start off where he finished.

Today there are research developments in the field and various attempts are being made to find the perfect artificial heart. In 1994 at St Vincent's, the first implantable LVAD (a partially artificial heart) was used. Fifteen of these have now been implanted into patients. Some of these patients have lived for up to one year while they wait for a donor heart. But the LVAD is very expensive and St Vincent's use of the device is limited by budgetary constraints.

Most of the work in this area over the last few years has been in America. I think if Dad were alive, he'd still be working on this project to produce a low-cost artificial heart for use in Australia and in Asia.

As for the St Vincent's valve, extensive trials did take place leading to implantation in more than 1000 patients in China, with acceptable results. A manufacturing company was established in Guandong Province. The final stages of production and quality control took place in Singapore, however, unfortunately, Singaporean surgeons didn't endorse its use. Dad's zeal and drive had helped promote the valve in developing countries but with his death, it went no further.

11

Goodbyes

I wanted this tribute to be about my father's life, not his death. Ironically, though, the catalyst for my decision to write a tribute were the thousands of letters my family received in the weeks and months after his death. The letters came from people around the nation and from all over the world, from ordinary people to high-profile members of the community, from patients and their families to scrub nurses, fellow doctors, students and carpark attendants, members of my family, friends and politicians. They told me the story of his life and they represent what I never knew before he died, how much love and respect he commanded from the people of Australia and Asia. I would like to share some of them.

These letters are personal and very precious to my family; each one is its own special tribute to Dad. For six months after he died my life was a blur. Something had gone terribly wrong, something I didn't understand then, and will probably never understand. For months, reading these letters was the only thing I looked forward to when I woke up in the morning. They helped support my family and provided us with a level of comfort that words can't explain.

Before I started work on this book, I set myself the task of reading each letter and each card, every single one, all over again, every day, all day. It took me just over one week to do it, including Saturday and Sunday. If I could, I would publish them all, indeed, I have incorporated some in the body of the book for fear that I would not be able to include them in this final chapter. After culling many thousands of letters down to just 200, I realised that this alone could fill a book. I reluctantly cut the number down further to only 83 this time and, still, there were so many words, beautiful words. I could not possibly include them all. To be able to do justice to the writers of these letters, I stopped at just under 30 letters and even then I could only include excerpts from most of them. Since I had to cut out large portions, I have added a short commentary to some of the letters to put them in context.

The sentiment may be the same for all the letters, but each one tells a unique story. This is my opportunity to thank all those people who wrote to my family in a most harrowing time. I hope you understand that I couldn't include every letter but I would like you to know that we treasure each one.

I also asked my mother and brothers Matthew and Marcus to write down their thoughts so I could include a personal contribution from them in this book. When I read what my brothers had written, each one intimate in its own way, I was reluctant to change what they had written by incorporating it within the body of the book. Therefore, I have left each contribution as a separate piece at the very end of the letters. There is also a final dedication from me, something I wrote many years ago for the embossed plaque at the memorial park opposite that place where my father spent so much of his life, St Vincent's Hospital. His ashes are buried under the dedication.

There is another institution opposite the plaque, the Victor Chang Cardiac Research Institute. One of Dad's attributes was his ability to share and implement his visions and to make them come true. That is why, since his death, many people have worked so hard and earnestly to make the Victor Chang Cardiac Research Institute a reality and a great force for research in areas Dad envisioned valuable progress. The Institute was opened on 1 November 1996 by Princess Diana as a research facility for the fundamental research into heart disease, one committed to providing excellence in cardiovascular research training and in facilitating the rapid application of research discoveries to patient care. There have already been two major discoveries by researchers at the Institute, both gene related. One is the discovery of the genetic defect that causes holes in the heart; the other is the discovery of the gene responsible for abnormal cell growth.

The cost of keeping the doors of the Institute open

each year is $5 million. Your purchase of this book has already helped raise funds for the Institute.

Finally, I think it is appropriate to let my father have the last say by including his answer to the question of what he would best like to be remembered for. He would have wanted this.

Letters from colleagues

I had the privilege of being one of [Victor's] residents in the Cameron Wing for three months in 1980. I found him to be an enormously attractive man and his warmth, his skill and personal charm made a great impression on me. I learnt more from him than from any other surgeon I worked with as a resident.

Allan Passmore, NSW

One of Dad's former residents and, in later years, the secretary-general of the Australian Medical Association, Allan Passmore regarded Dad as a mentor.

I had the honour [of serving] as your father's RMO in 1976 at St Vincent's Hospital and I developed a great love of Victor's surgical skill and good humour. Many times he was able to break the stress and tension of a difficult situation in theatre by his dexterity with his hands and his quick wit.

It was a welcome relief for us as RMOs when Victor would 'scrub in' to give one of the other surgeons or the Registrars a hand, because we knew then that the case would get finished quickly and we could all relax together.

He was a great one for taking the team out to a lavish Chinese banquet in Goulburn Street . . .

John Garvey, NSW

This letter from John Garvey gives an insight into the atmosphere inside the operating theatre.

I was honoured to have known Victor even longer than you, from the days of his residency at St Vincent's. Over the years I got to know him as a brilliant surgeon, bio-engineer and a wonderfully warm, kind, caring human being. Over the last seventeen years I have been involved with his many overseas patients, at his request, from a voluntary social work point of view Victor gave of himself unsparingly and gave hope to the hopeless. Many accolades were bestowed on him we know, but I think the greatest tribute to him is made by the gratitude, respect, and . . . love that came from the thousands of 'little people' who owe their very existence to his devotion to humanity. Without fear or favour, regardless or race, colour, or creed, he did all that he could for everyone.

Smiley Adcock, QLD

'Smiley' Adcock was responsible for looking after overseas families, on a voluntary basis, and he *was* always smiling, hence the nickname. Dad liked him a lot; he would often leave me in Smiley's care, and I would look forward to our time together.

I was working as an 'old timer' nurse at Cameron Wing when Victor arrived and he was ever helpful to all of us, cheerful and supportive. Also I appreciated the fact that when I became a patient there he visited me when he had a few spare minutes.

He never cut off what a patient was saying to him— he listened. This alone made his patients feel comfortable apart from all his other great talents.

Of course, this was years ago but my abiding memory is when we would all be squashed into the tea room on the fourth floor. You would be just about able to swing a poor old cat in it, if so inclined. I can so vividly see Victor, green theatre cap pushed back, smiling, chatting and enjoying his tea. That great spirit will never disappear.

Maureen Gordons

This letter brings back memories for me. Cameron Wing was one of the older parts of St Vincent's, and no longer exists. When I was doing rounds with Dad, he would deposit me in the Cameron Wing tea room to munch on biscuits while he examined patients. Sometimes he would take such a long time that I'd dress up as a surgeon and use syringes as water pistols to keep myself entertained!

I very much enjoyed my association with Victor over the years. He had a nice sense of humour and seemed to enjoy life with the enthusiasm and pleasure of a child.

I used to tease him sometimes and say, 'Victor how does it feel to be so rich and famous?' He would give me a very serious and earnest look and say in a [deprecating] way, 'No no, I'm not.' I liked that.

Marguerite Weston, NSW

I laughed when I read this letter from one of Dad's colleagues, it was so typical of Dad to deny his achievements. I think modesty was one of his most admirable qualities.

It is difficult for me to see him as the famous cardiac surgeon he became when I remember him above all as a bouncy super-efficient SHO at the Brompton in 1969! (. . . I was there as an anaesthetic senior registrar before I went to Oxford.) . . . I still think nostalgically of the [Chang] home vintage wine that improved the Brompton residents' meals!

Jane Baker (Colliss), Dunedin, NZ

The 'human' side of Dad is illustrated here—he was just a man after all—but it was reassuring to read this letter. Dad never drank wine. If he did, he would break out in hives, so I found this letter amusing.

I worked with Victor in the private hospital intensive care unit for thirteen years. I can still recall my amazement, when starting at SVPH [St Vincent's Public Hospital], at the rapid recovery of Victor's patients and the ease of their post-operative management. I must have repeated on hundreds of occasions since then, when new staff have expressed their incredulousness, what had been told me, that it was due to the skill of the surgeon. While most of us were used to working in units where at least two or three patients a week returned to theatre with complications, I would be surprised if we had one of Victor's patients return to theatre in my first year there.

I thought Victor was just wonderful. I have always been proud to say I work with him and to espouse his brilliance and altruism. He had so much enthusiasm which couldn't help but inspire us all no matter how busy, stressful or tragic the unit was, the atmosphere brightened on Victor's arrival. He had such a sparkle in his eyes and I can still hear this beautiful laugh . . .

Victor had many exceptional qualities, not least of which were his thoughtfulness and generosity. Whilst many tributes have been paid to Victor through the press, from his patients and colleagues, I would like to emphasise his consideration and benevolence towards his nurses. Victor had outstanding leadership skills, and a quality rarely found in surgeons of making nurses feel worthwhile. Not only did he always take the time to thank us, even though he would have worked twice as hard and for twice as long, we were always enjoying scrumptious Chinese meals, with compliments of Victor.

Penny Frost, NSW

I am a scrub sister at St Vincent's Public Hospital and . . . worked very closely with Victor [for four] years. I learned so much from him—shared his expertise, his knowledge, his determination. I learned the meaning of dedication, commitment, getting the best out of myself—he taught that very well. I learned the feeling of giving life to someone else when all looked like it was lost . . .

He was a dear friend, a mentor, an inspiration—the energy he inspired kept things turning over. He was generous—if you asked for it you usually got it . . . he liked to reward courage with recognition. He could be a real tyrant at times, and knew how to push buttons in you that would really test your own strengths and weaknesses.

Another big lesson I learned from Victor Chang was never look back, what is past is past, to live is to live now, be thankful for what you already have, you never make mistakes, merely create challenges, throughout your life.

Ronnie

Letters from public figures

Although I did not know your husband very well, we were aware of each other's particular relationship and I recall so vividly sharing with him, as you did, the great joy when he was invested with the Companionship of the Order of Australia on the same day as I was appointed to the Order in Canberra.

As a former member of the Board of the Royal North Shore Hospital for over twenty years and a heart surgery patient . . . I was aware of the tremendous respect in which he was held not merely as a great and skilled surgeon but as a warm-hearted human being ever prepared to share his God-given gifts with others.

The Hon. Sir Asher Joel, KBE, AO, NSW

Dad and Asher Joel didn't know one another well but shared a mutual respect. Sadly, both have now passed away.

Your husband has been a great inspiration to me not simply because he was a gifted surgeon, but especially because he so actively took his services to parts of the world where such skills and benefits were not readily available.

His efforts in China have been an inspiration to our much smaller work in spreading modern eye surgery to the less advantaged places on earth.

F.C. Hollows, AC, MB, ChB (NZ), DO (LOND), FRCS, FRACO, MD Hon (UNSW), DSc Hon (Macq), NSW

It is a great tribute to my father to have received this letter from the late, brilliant Fred Hollows.

Dr Chang's contribution to medicine was recognised worldwide. Many Australian and people throughout the region owe their lives to his enormous skill, dedication and commitment.

It was for his contribution to medicine and to the development of cardiac surgery in China and South East Asia that Victor was awarded the Companion of the Order of Australia in 1986.

His will be a great loss, not only to his colleagues in the medical field, but to all Australians who value excellence and Victor's outstanding contribution to his country.

R.J.L. Hawke, Prime Minister, Canberra ACT

I met Victor many years ago. He had enlisted my help and that of others in his important fund-raising activities. I was honoured to play a very small part in his most significant work. Even then, he had the stamp of greatness, and as events later were to prove, he was indeed a very special man.

It has been my experience that the very best among us are always taken from us when they are far too young to go. That is certainly true in Victor's case.

Ita Buttrose, AO, OBE, NSW

The second paragraph in this letter from Ita Buttrose struck a sad chord with me.

Letters from patients

Dr Chang saved my life, years ago at St Vincent's and he will always be remembered for his precise efficiency and his dedication to his patients.

There was always a very kind smile behind the surgical face mask together with the frankness of his eyes looking straight at you. Those were the eyes of a very pure soul and a very active and logical mind.

Patrick de Vienne, NSW

Dad did have lovely, kind eyes and more often than not he'd be wearing that surgical mask, so this image of him is a familiar one.

When my husband (John Sheath) went back to see Dr Chang after his op for his check-up, I went with him. After he had examined him [my husband] I said to Dr Chang, 'Tell me doctor, the book that all patients are given telling them what to do and when, surely it had to be written by a man?' And he, with a serious look on face, said, 'Why do you ask that?' I said, 'Because they can't go fishing for so many weeks, can't pick up a tea towel for eight weeks, yet it states that they can get back to a normal sex life in about six weeks. That's why I say it had to be written by a man.' He said, 'That's right, I only operate on the top half.'

With that I burst out laughing and said, 'I'm only joking.' And he got the giggles too. As we were leaving his surgery, he looked me in the eye and said to both of us with a grin on his beautiful face, shook our hands and said, 'Enjoy your sex life.'

Audrey Sheath, NSW

Within this little anecdote is a classic example of Dad's sense of humour, which many of the letters have mentioned but not exemplified. I know this story to be true.

Victor was one of the team of surgeons who performed open-heart surgery on my husband seventeen years ago and it was his quick response to a complication that saved Fred's life—something that we are all so grateful for and shall never forget.

The warmth and affection portrayed to me as he held my hands and explained what he was going to do remains, today, as if it was only yesterday.

Margaret and Fred, NSW

Mum was first operated on at St Vincent's by Mr Harry Windsor in 1959, the first of many operations to follow over the years. She talked of a wonderful young man (one of Harry Windsor's [protégés]) . . . Mum had five lots of major surgery four of these performed by Dr Chang, and the last of these in 1974 . . . The last two operations we knew were dangerous, and that the 'Panel' did not want to do, but Dr Chang insisted in taking up the challenge, for a [long-time] friend, and Thank God he did—as he and the others gave us another [nine] years to love and care for her. Mum considered Dr Chang the nearest thing to a Saint that man can be.

Margaret and Dan Gregory, QLD

[While] I was in St Vincent's some thirteen years ago [Victor] operated on two penniless people; a boy from Hong Kong and a youth from Singapore, both with very serious heart ailments—they were of course both successful and all this was done without any charge whatsoever to these two very grateful people whom I got to know well.

Gerald Fitzgerald, NSW

I have mentioned that I admired Dad's modesty, another quality of his was altruism, with no expectation of reward for it. When I read this letter, I felt proud that Dad extended his generosity in this way to many overseas patients.

There is no doubt Victor was 'one of a kind', a dedicated, brilliant and compassionate surgeon who was without peer. I will be forever grateful to him for

*performing a most difficult quadruple by-pass on me
on 9 June 1981 and giving me ten years of
worthwhile life.*

*Victor was a most charming self-effacing person and
made his patients totally at ease even in the face of
major surgery and I believe gave his patients a
confidence not usually felt with other medical people.*

John Murkin, NSW

The ability to inspire hope and trust in a person about
to undergo major surgery was a theme that ran
through many letters from Dad's patients.

*Our son James had surgery in St Vincent's on 12 May
1977 for a narrowing of his aorta. He was nineteen
years old and eldest of six children . . . We met and
spoke with Dr [Chang] the night before the operation
and he explained all and then asked if we had any
questions. I said, 'No, we know all will go well and he's
in God's hands.' 'No' Dr [Chang] replied, 'He's in my
hands.' He held them up and we all laughed.*

Don and Babe Connell, NSW

I loved reading letters from patients and their families
about operations that had been carried out decades
ago. They told me that Dad had done a good job.

I met Dr Chang when he did my mum's heart transplant . . . I will never forget when he rang to tell me that they were doing her. My husband said that Dr Chang was on the phone and I didn't believe him, but it was him telling me what was going on . . . the day after the operation [I] went to shake his hand. Not knowing I went to squeeze and he pulled away and said 'No, like this.' His hands were just like a baby's skin, so soft.

My mum went to the funeral and it is custom for Aboriginal people to touch the coffin and bless them. I believe she did it as her respect for Victor.

Judy Norris, Galba via Cobargo, NSW

I particularly identified with this letter because Judy mentions the soft skin on Dad's hands, something that I always remember with great fondness.

I am in my last year at Christian Brothers High School Lewisham, and we have almost completed our trial examinations for our HSC and I have been busy studying.

My parents and I first met Dr Chang when I was only [two] years old and now I'm eighteen. After many years of testing, at the age of [nine] I was operated on in St Vincent's Hospital . . . Dr Chang was unaware whether or not this would be my first and hopefully last operation . . . there [were] no guarantees.

Well, after [three and a half] weeks in hospital, about

six months off school and [nine] years later I'm over 6 feet tall and fit as a fiddle, so to speak, thanks to your husband, my friend and doctor, Dr Chang.

Michael Berenger, NSW

Please know that your husband has twice saved my life, first in January, 1976 . . . I was admitted to St Vincent's Cardiac Ward on December 22, 1975, but, because the [bypass] unit had dispersed for the Christmas vacation, my operation was postponed. Dr Chang told me that he and his family were going off for a holiday for a week or so, but that I would be operated on first thing in the New Year. He was a fibber, you know! He was back in the ward within [three or four] days. 'Just keeping an eye on things,' he said, and he in fact spent quite long periods doing just that. He sat on his patients' beds, including my own, and talked, and together several of us watched TV . . . but we knew that he was with us because he was a very caring person. My operation was carried out early in January, 1976, and, as you see, was a success.

Eleven years later, after a possible (third) heart attack, I was again referred to your husband. This time, he told me, the chances of success were lower but, if I chose, he would 'do' me. Having the greatest faith in him, I chose and he 'did' me, and again, as you see nearly five years later, the operation was successful.

Noel V. Riggs, ACT

Noel's story says a lot about the comfort that my father found in simply being around the hospital. It wasn't a job for him, it was his life.

My name in 1980 was Ann Reed and to my knowledge I was the first person Dr Chang assessed for a heart transplant . . . therefore, I am truly aware of just how hard Victor worked to establish the centre, a task [that] could not have been achieved without the support of a loving and understanding family. I finally had my transplant in 1987 and the memory [of] Victor's beaming face as he introduced me to two Chinese visiting professors as the lady who started it all will always stay fresh with me. He was so compassionate and proud of us all as we were of him and his dedicated team. I resumed [full-time] work four months after receiving my new lease on life . . .

Ann Rathbone, QLD

Dad had many opportunities to 'show off' the heart transplant patients; he was proud of all of them.

Letters from friends

In this world we live in, the world that is capable of the magic of the music of Mozart and Beethoven, the glorious colours of the painters Monet and Sisley, the first light of the day kissing the hills and splashing showers of gold about and into the valleys below and to see the cattle solid and calm looking at the new day in their wonderful dumb way, the flapping of wings of the alert crow so black in body in the early morning light—this was the world we shared this friend of mine.

He was a lovely man and man so kind and [skilful], he cared and healed in the world of the sick and even when he spoke to you or touched you, you felt as though something special had been added to your life, so warming was his gift.

He was known worldwide for his skills in his field of medicine and his kindness, but as one of the very lucky ones [who] managed to cross his path and become his friend, you knew that with him no matter how famous he became, no matter if he was talking to kings and queens, you knew if you had to call him because of your troubles he would leave and come to your aid.

We shared a mutual passion for cars and I can see him now flipping through a car magazine I offered him, looking down through his glasses and up at me again with his impish grin . . . and then we would both laugh. The magazines and the car talk we both loved [were] the plank of our friendship.

So to the desperadoes . . . you may have snuffed out the mortal life of my friend Victor—you may have taken from me the touch of his hand the grin and so many joys we shared in this world together, but you will never snuff out the memories he left me, because I was one of the very lucky ones . . . so fortunate to cross his path.

As I know and believe there is a god in heaven he will be greeted with great love. He was my friend.

Keith Boyd, NSW

This letter from Keith Boyd who ran our local newsagency for ten years was one of the most touching. Dad would drive one of his cars up to the newsagency every Sunday morning to buy the weekend papers. This letter, published almost in full, always brings tears to my eyes.

It is many years since we met; the occasion of your arrival in Australia. I remember the day well, with its anguish and trauma . . . Dad trying desperately to sort the Health Department problems out. However, my memories of [Victor] go back even further. I remember him on the front verandah at the old family house in the early 1960s, drawing me pictures of aeroplanes. Little did I know then that my life would be aviation and my last meeting with Victor would be aboard a Qantas jet.

Words can never offer enough at this time but I am sure my father would want me to say something at least. He would have been devastated to hear of such a tragic event. He knew his work was in safe hands when he died.

Hugh Windsor, NSW

This is a letter from Harry Windsor's son, Hugh, reminiscing about the day my family arrived in Australia in 1972. My brother Matthew was whisked off to quarantine from the airport, a rather dramatic introduction to this country!

It really is remarkable how much [Victor] had achieved by 54 years of age, and nothing can take that away . . . he was always so natural about his achievements also. We will retain such very happy memories. We remember . . . our stay with you at Rochester, Minn, and again with you in your house in Sydney. I could go on for a very long time . . .

A.Y. Mason, London

[Victor] is laughing above here in heaven right now and of that I am certain—I can almost hear him say in his own, inimitable way, 'Gee Catherine it's good to be here!'

Catherine Hally, Surrey, UK

This letter is from Catherine Hally, the Sister at St Anthony's who played cupid with Mum and Dad back in 1966.

Letters from the public

Like most people, I have never met nor even seen Dr Chang in person, but I have heard much of him. As an Australian-born Chinese, I always felt extremely proud of Dr Chang and his achievements. I was born here but lived almost 30 years in China. When I was back on a visit to Peking earlier this year I met an old friend of mine, Mr Yao Zhao Hui, who told me he had just returned from Singapore where he had had a bypass operation performed by Dr Chang. Mr Yao told me when Dr Chang [learnt] he had been in China for 40 years working and had no money of his own (the Communist government pays only a pittance to its workers and intellectuals) and his brothers were to pay the expenses, he waived his fee and performed the operation for nothing. I was deeply moved by Dr Chang's understanding and compassion for someone he did not know.

Pamela Tan, ACT

I know precisely where I stood in a prisoner-of-war camp when the death of President Roosevelt was announced. Even the German guards saluted his memory. I know precisely where I was when the death of President Kennedy was announced.

But nothing in my life compares with the death of [Victor Chang]. I am not ashamed to say that I wept at the announcement of his death. And even more so when I heard your daughter [Vanessa] proclaim the eulogy.

I am ashamed for Australia.

Doug Benbow, SA

I was listening to the 7 pm news a few moments ago and I was privileged to hear your moving and touching eulogy at your father's funeral. I am a sensitive person and like many others around this nation tears came out of my eyes.

The closest I've been to heart surgery has been an angioplasty balloon operation five years ago for angina. Thanks to that and medication I am now a healthy person.

I have always appreciated what the medical profession has done for me and countless others, I respect them as angels not yet in heaven.

I felt revulsion and anger last week when I heard over the news the loss of your wonderful father. Whoever makes life's rules has made them tough when they take people such as your father . . .

Please excuse the writing as I am on duty till midnight and am half in, half out of my car in poor light. I grieve so much for you all, God Bless.

Norm Brown, WA

A security guard sitting in his car at a city carpark put pen to paper to write this letter to me.

Matthew Chang

At last, it had arrived. 'Mum's not gonna like this!' said Dad, grinning from ear to ear and giggling like Mutley, the dog in the 'Wacky Races' cartoons. Dad had always loved cars and this time it was a new burgundy Porsche 911 Carrera Turbo. For months the Porsche dealer in the city (Dale Goodman) had been persuading him to buy a car. 'You'll look good in this, Vic,' he'd said. I don't think he really liked the cars that stood out too much, like Ferraris, because they drew too much attention, but Dale had sent him off to the Porsche driving school and now he had to have one.

It's very sad looking back and hearing stories about Dad and realising now how similar we were to each other, even though we never spent much time together. Dad was always busy at the hospital, so we never had much quality time together.

He loved his work; it was his life. He worked from very early in the morning until late at night almost every day except Sunday. We always wanted to play tennis with him when he had the time, but he could never play as he had to operate the next day and he didn't want his hands to be shaking. Most of the time his Saturdays would be spent at work doing the rounds and Sunday would be taken up with washing his cars and watching sport on TV.

Even now as I build my model planes in the garage and wonder if I can make a model Harrier jet actually fly I hear stories of my Dad when he was young, when he was doing exactly the same things in his garage—working on jet engines, remote-controlled planes and cars. I guess I was too young to recognise or understand these similarities in the way he and I think.

My liking for electronics regularly got me in trouble and always caused arguments with Dad. He would bring home the latest, greatest, state-of-the-art electronics equipment from Hong Kong and hide it away somewhere upstairs in his study. True to form, I would have to explore and, once the new purchase had been located, I would proceed to dismantle it, whether it was a new hi-fi system, or the latest video cassette recorder. I can see his face now filled with rage, looking at me in disbelief as he would enter the room to see the nuts, bolts, circuit boards and LCD displays neatly laid out on the carpet for me to examine. I would always be insisting that it would be easy to fix and they always did go back together. But because of my inquisitive mechanical nature and history of offences like this, I was always blamed for anything that was broken in the house!

Once, when I was nine years old, we were on holiday in Surfers Paradise. It was Christmas and I had been given a new glider with big blue foam wings and a plastic body. The wings finally snapped from continually flying it around the room of the hotel, so I had to fix them. An argument erupted as Dad tried to show me how to fix the wings. I insisted he wasn't going to succeed using his method and that he should listen to me; he was insisting just the opposite. Shortly after losing our little battle I watched as Dad proceeded to glue the wings back together. We built the next model, the 'Trident 2000', together.

It would have been nice to grow old with Dad and I think we would have been great friends as I grew older and more mature. He would have begun to understand me and I him.

I will never forget one night, which was perhaps the strangest night of my life. Soon to turn 21, my relationship with my father was strained at the best of times. It had been a long time since we had been nice to each other. This was probably due to the fact that I didn't have a job and he could see me wasting my time. Dad had always insisted that I go to university and I was always adamant that it would be the last thing I would ever do. I went to pilot school instead.

That afternoon I received a call from my good buddy, Debbie. We had known each other for many years. She had rung to invite herself around for a dinner with the Changs. In all these years of being my friend, she had only briefly met my dad on the driveway, so she wanted to come over to meet him and have dinner with us.

Dad arrived home from work and Debbie finally met him. We were all having dinner together and at the time I can remember feeling very odd. For the first time in a long time, Dad and I were actually laughing together. When dinner was over this continued. Dad, Debbie and I went down into our courtyard area together to play with Lucy, our beagle. We sat on the step and laughed and chatted, and laughed again. I think we were laughing at the dog.

It felt very strange when Dad put his arm around my shoulder as we laughed, like a friend would. It was the evening of 3 July 1991 and I would never see my father again.

Marcus Chang

When Ness first asked me to write down something about Dad, I was scared at the thought. I guess I feared that bringing up the past would only make me sadder for the times I think I should have done more.

I remember spending a lot of time with Dad as a young child. I don't know if it was because I was the youngest or the naughtiest, but there was a period when Dad used to take me to work every weekend for years. My brother and sister were going along too and soon got sick of it. They must have said something to Mum and they got out of it, but I stayed on.

I have vivid memories about doing rounds and visiting Dad's 'cases' every Saturday and sometimes Sunday. Dad was always on duty, always had his pager close by and was only ever half an hour's drive from the hospital. The usual day would start off by greeting everyone. Dad knew everyone's first name no matter who they were—the cleaner, the carpark attendant or the cafeteria workers. We would then venture to his office in the medical centre, pick up some papers and head off to the rooms.

When we arrived at each patient, Dad would ask the sister in charge if anything was unusual. More often than not he would sit on their bed talking about the operation they had just received. Dad would then ask the patient to perform some basic movement skills. He talked to them, he didn't just ask them questions, he really got to know them. Even the families, if they were present, were allowed to stay and watch Dad 'weave his magic'. The family members would not be spared question time either. He made people laugh and joked accordingly. He had a great bedside manner, a human touch.

Only recently has this become apparent to me. My Dad loved people, he loved saving people's lives to give them another go, to finish what would have normally been cut short. I hear of stories where my father operated on cases that he was advised not to because the patient may have been too old or too sick, but he took calculated risks. He loved helping people especially if they were 'battlers'.

I'm sure I can add more to this story or integrate other stories but I do find it a little disturbing and it makes me sad. I miss my father dearly. I miss the smell of the hospital that I used to smell when he came home at night. I miss him as a friend. I miss him as a father, someone to give guidance to a son. I miss seeing him cleaning his car on the weekend, which was his only exercise besides walking around many hospital corridors. There are a lot of things I miss about this great man but life has to go on.

'Going on' was a common theme from the many letters I received from family, friends and strangers whom Dad had touched in some way or form. I don't want to believe it but I have to. To know that one day many of my unanswered questions will be answered is good enough.

I would encourage anyone who knew my father or

who was touched by my father's work to say hello next time they meet a member of the Chang family. I'm hoping it will be at a fundraising event for the VCCRI (Victor Chang Cardiac Research Institute) but if it's not it should be bearable. It's good therapy as long as the timing is right.

A final dedication

Isn't time amazing? How the years slip away. Suddenly and sadly you are only a memory now and finally I have found the time to sit down and write this dedication to you. I admit I *have* procrastinated, perhaps because this is a tangible affirmation that you are gone, something that has taken me a long, long time to accept.

Where are you now? We all thought you were immortal. People still approach me and say, 'I'm so sorry about your father, he was a great man,' and I think, 'My God you're never coming back are you?'

You know, I play that day—4 July 1991—back to myself in my mind all the time. I ask myself, 'Why? Why didn't you resist and put up a fight, Dad? Why didn't you let those men get what they wanted and walk away? Were you in any pain when they took your life away? I pray that you died peacefully, with no pain; this is something that will haunt me for the rest of my life. I know you are peaceful now.

I always wonder why you have never visited me or left some sort of sign to say that we'll meet again one day. Matt says he always dreams about you, that he speaks to you in his dreams, but you are only a ghost to me.

In the evenings when I hear the turn of the key in the front door, I close my eyes and expect to see you walk through that door and feel the pat of your hand on my head. I close my eyes and hear your voice echo in the kitchen, is that Dad talking in there? Then, to my disappointment, I realise it's someone else's voice. I close my eyes and smell hospital corridors on your shirts that now belong to your sons. I still see scraps of your handwriting on cards and notes that are buried in my drawers. I remember the skin on your surgeon's hands, made soft through years of careful washing. I sometimes look in the mirror and see traces of your face staring back at me—a smile, a frown—the image of her father. I still believe that one day you'll call me to say that it was all a mistake and that you're coming home.

Not one day has passed without me thinking of you, I expect I always will. Sometimes I burn a candle for you in St Mary's Cathedral, and I cry. I realise that we only loved you as any family would love their father, while your patients saw you as their saviour, a miracle worker.

Every piece of writing has a time and a purpose and this isn't a time for eulogising.

From your death I have learnt that greed distorts and destroys. Each life is a precious and often fragile thing; taste it, smell it, touch it, laugh at it, embrace it. Appreciate little moments; make the most of what you have; savour each memory; tell the people you love that you love them, all the time, not just when something goes wrong. Have compassion for others; make your time worthwhile.

Life must be celebrated; death will be mourned. But, as Mum always says, life must go on. Besides, I have my memories and when I miss you I just close my eyes.

Victor Chang, what would you best like to be remembered for?

I can't really answer that. I feel that I have still quite a few years to go. I would like to contribute a lot more before I finish. I don't want to go down in history as a great contributor, but I would like to do something that would be very beneficial to the community for a long time.

For example, I would like to develop a heart valve of my own design or to refine the development of a totally implantable artificial heart. I would very much like to be part of the development of the artificial heart, I think it would be really great if it can be done in an Asian community so that at least we can show that we, too, can contribute to major development in the medical profession.

Chronology
1936–1991

1936 On 21 November, Dad is born Chang Yam Him and given the English name Victor Peter Chang, in Shanghai, China, son of Aubrey Chang and May Chang (nee Lee).

1938 The Chang family moves to Hong Kong (Kowloon) after the Japanese invasion of Shanghai. Sister Frances is born.

1940 As tensions between China and Japan flare up once again, the Chang family leaves Hong Kong bound for Rangoon, Burma, where Aubrey is waiting for them. Brother Anthony is born.

1941 The Japanese bomb Rangoon and the family travels east along the Burma Road to Yunnan

Province in south-west China, where they stay for several months. On this trip, they lose all their possessions when their transport lorry rolls over a steep cliff. After several months, they leave once more and head north to Chung King, China's wartime capital. Dad starts pre-school at the age of five.

1945   The Japanese surrender and the family returns to Kowloon Tong in Hong Kong. Dad attends Kowloon Tong Primary School.

1948   Dad nurses his mother who is diagnosed with breast cancer. However, on 7 April—after a long battle—May Chang dies in Australia. The children are in Hong Kong when this happens. At twelve years of age, Dad decides he wants to be a doctor.

1950   Dad attends St Paul's Boys College in Bonham Road in Hong Kong, where he meets Peter Lee. The two boys share a passion for making model aeroplanes and cars. Dad's school grades are average.

The Korean War erupts.

1951   Aubrey decides to send Dad and Frances to Australia to live with Aubrey's older brother, Charlie, and his family in Campsie, Sydney. Dad attends a local school.

1952   Dad meets Pearl Hansen, Frances' school friend.

1953   Frances returns to Hong Kong on 25 August after spending a miserable time in Sydney. Dad remains as he is not finding it so hard to adjust to his new environment. He moves from the local school, as it does not provide enough challenge for him, to the Christian Brothers College in Lewisham.

1954   Due to arguments between Dad and Charlie's two sons, Dad moves to Punchbowl to live with Aubrey's sister, Fung—Dad's Sixth Aunt—and his Uncle Reg and their family.

1955   Dad passes his Leaving Certificate and is accepted into the University of Sydney to study medicine.

1956   First year medicine. Dad is awarded the Commonwealth of Australia Scholarship, which he is awarded every year throughout his university education.

1957   Second year medicine. Dad is awarded the Prosectorship Prize in Anatomy. He meets Michael Allam.

1958   Third year medicine. Dad meets Sister Bernice when he begins his clinical training at St Vincent's Hospital in Darlinghurst. On 1 March he celebrates his 21st birthday at his Uncle Les's house in Seaforth.

1959 Fourth year medicine. In mid 1959 Dad moves to Epiphany House, a boys' hostel in Neutral Bay, Sydney. He works at the local supermarket, packing shelves, to earn extra money.

1960 In March he moves to Wesley College on the campus of the University of Sydney. He decides, after meeting Michael Rand, to interrupt his medical degree to undertake a year of medical research. He graduates with a Bachelor of Science (Med), First Class Honours, and is awarded the Medical Research Foundation Scholarship and the Boots (Aust) Ltd Research Scholarship. He publishes four articles. Later that year, he moves to a cottage in the grounds of St Vincent's.

1961 Fifth year medicine.

1962 On 20 January he is admitted to degrees of Bachelor of Medicine and Bachelor of Surgery (Distinction in surgery).

1963 First year resident medical officer (junior) at St Vincent's Hospital, working in casualty for six months, then general surgery for six months. He attends a lecture given by cardiac surgeon Dr Mark Shanahan, and approaches Mark after his talk to express his desire to follow in Mark's footsteps.

1964 Senior resident medical officer at St Vincent's.

He meets cardiac surgeon, Dr Harry Windsor. First he works for six months in surgery, then six months in the Department of Thoracic Surgery.

1965   Surgical registrar to cardio-thoracic unit. In September Dad leaves for England to take up a position as senior house officer and surgical registrar at St Anthony's Catholic Hospital in Cheam, Surrey, assisting the general surgeon, Dr Aubrey York Mason. On 8 November Dad obtains FRCS (Fellowship of Royal College of Surgeons).

1966   Dad meets and diagnoses a patient, Ann Simmons, with tonsillitis. Later that year, he moves to another role as surgical registrar, again, to Aubrey York Mason at St Helier Hospital, Carshalton, Surrey.

1967   In December, Dr Christiaan Barnard performs the world's first human-to-human heart transplant in Capetown, South Africa.

1968   On 20 April, Dad marries Ann Simmons. In October he starts at Brompton Chest Clinic as Surgical Registrar under Lord Brock.
October—The first heart transplant in Australia is performed on Richard Pye at St Vincent's Hospital, Sydney, by Dr Harry Windsor.

1969   On 28 May, Vanessa is born in Surrey.

1970   On 13 October, Matthew is born in Surrey. In December the Chang family moves to the United States, to live in Rochester, Minnesota, where Dad continues his thoracic training at the Mayo Clinic, working under Dwight McGoon.

1972   In January Dad brings his family to Sydney. He takes up the role as staff cardiac surgeon working alongside Dr Harry Windsor and Dr Mark Shanahan at St Vincent's Hospital. Our family moves into a small unit at Manly.

1973   Dad obtains FRACS (Fellowship of the Royal Australasian College of Surgeons).

1974   In April he assists Harry and Mark in Australia's second heart transplant. The patient dies after 62 days and the heart transplant program is temporarily put on hold.
         In May, Marcus is born in Sydney.

1975   Dad obtains FACS (Fellowship of the American College of Surgeons).

1977   He visits China for the first time in three decades.

1978   The first visiting Chinese doctors come to Australia to train under Dad and the team at St Vincent's.

1979 Cyclosporin A is first used.

1980 Dad is appointed Honorary Professor of Surgery, Chinese Academy of Medical Sciences, Beijing, China. He begins research work on producing a low-cost artificial heart valve for use in the Asia-Pacific region. Eventually the valve is manufactured and implanted in 1000 patients in China.

1982 In June, the Australian Government recommends that a national heart transplant unit be set up in Australia.

1983 In December, federal and state Health ministers announce that St Vincent's will house the first heart transplant unit and Dad is selected as its Director. He is appointed as Honorary Professor of Surgery, Shanghai Second Medical School, Shanghai, China; appointed as Honorary Professor, Xian University Medical School; appointed as Honorary Director of Heart, Lung and Blood Vessel Research Institute, Quandong Provincial Peoples Hospital, Quanzhou, China.

1984 In February, Dad performs the first heart transplant in Australia since 1974. The patient is Neville Apthorpe. Approximately five weeks later, Dad gives Fiona Coote her first new heart.

1985   Dad is Visiting Professor Cardiothoracic Surgery, National University of Singapore. He receives the Advance Australia Award—Australian of the Year. He sets up the research team for work on the development of an artificial heart.

1986   Dad performs the first heart–lung transplant. In March he receives the Companion of the Order of Australia (AC) for 'service to international relations between Australia and China and to medical science'.

1987   Dad is Visiting Professor Cardiothoracic Surgery, National Cardiac Centre, Jakarta, Indonesia.

1988   On 16 May, Dad is awarded an honorary degree from the University of NSW.

1990   Fifth prototype of the artificial heart is ready for clinical testing.

1991   4 July—Dad's life is taken.

If you would like to visit the Victor Chang Cardiac Research Insitute (VCCRI) website, it can be found at: www.victorchang.com.au

Donations to the VCCRI can be made by contacting:
The Fund Development Office
Level 4, 376 Victoria Street (PO Box 699)
Darlinghurst NSW 2010

Tel: (02) 8382 3022
Fax: (02) 8382 3585